D1546416

Praise for William Bradley and *Fractals*

In William Bradley's debut collection of essays, *Fractals,* we circle around topics as big and heavy as love, cancer, mortality, family and faith, but we approach them through the critical analysis and appreciation of comic book heroes, soap operas, music, books and pop culture. Bradley seduces the reader with humor and honesty, with a voice that is simultaneously playful and deeply serious. The book moves and grows, accreting meaning and depth as it patterns our experience of the author's life—always reaching for the heart through the mind. Bradley returns to certain subjects through different but self-similar windows, allowing the reader to experience a whole that is greater than the sum of its component parts. Smart, funny, heartbreaking, and captivating, *Fractals* is a must-read for lovers of essays.

Steven Church, author of *Ultrasonic: Essays;* founding editor of *The Normal School.*

William Bradley pays close attention to the world, from soap operas to David Bowie, from the intimacy of marriage to the shockwave of a cancer diagnosis. Thank goodness he does so, because the result is *Fractal*s, a brilliant constellation of personal essays revealing, in vivid prose and with just the perfect measure of wit, the extraordinary patterns that connect us all.

Dinty W. Moore, author of *Dear Mister Essay Writer Guy*

The outrageous mystery of *Fractals* is the way in which essays on suffering and doubt become so vividly and sweetly alive. William Bradley has urgent stuff to tell you about cancer but also about soap operas and love and horror movies—all without melodrama or the pretense of irony. Bradley is a boy grown into a man who finds solace in the pantheon of what he calls 'dorkiness' as he summons the imagined children of the future and ghost children of the past. These are the essays you are looking for.

Sonya Huber, author of *Opa Nobody* and *Cover Me: A Health Insurance Memoir*

In *Fractals* we find William Bradley facing experiences both trifling and troubling with grace and humility. He writes with equanimity and eloquence about horror movies and soap operas and chemotherapy and comic books and wavers of faith and doubt. There seems to be no limit to the oddities and profundities, nor to the insights and beauties. In *Fractals* we find William Bradley, yes, but here, too, we find ourselves.

Patrick Madden, author of *Quotidiana*

William Bradley deftly balances the ache of knowing the difficult truths of life with charm, laugh-out-loud humor, and grace. In a single turn, he can move from wrestling with the uncertainties built from loss to celebrating the ways in which what we loved then and what we love now are the real and true things that sustain us. Within these varied and vast contemplations of time, memory, faith, fear, death, regret, and the knowledge that the past is forever lost to us, Bradley ultimately urges us to continue to seek the best version of ourselves and to hold on to "what still might be."

Jill Talbot, author of *The Way We Weren't: A Memoir*

Fractals is an incisive, moving rumination on love and faith and identity in the face of illness, both personal and societal. William Bradley is a thrilling writer and a much-needed voice in contemporary American culture.

Michael Kardos, author of *Before He Finds Her*

William Bradley has an unerring ability to validate all the ephemera you ever suspected was important but didn't know why. *Fractals* considers subjects light and heavy, grotesque and sublime, but treats all of them with a discernment that challenges our assumptions about the relationships that bind people, culture and objects. The collection is humorous, moving and honest.

Michael Piafsky, author of *All the Happiness You Deserve*

Whether addressing matters concerning family, the imperfect art of growing up, love, the ravages of cancer, or one-way trips to Mars, William Bradley's pithy, incisive essays mine small moments that result in large consequences. *Fractals* is a collection of keen-eyed observations that are framed by the bigger picture of mortality. We're all on a one-way trip and William Bradley is determined to make the most of his; the result is a collection of essays that should come with not a warning but a recommendation: This is a book to be read to Warren Zevon's rendition of "Back in the Highlife," played on repeat mode.

John Smolens, author of *Quarantine* and *The Schoolmaster's Daughter*

Those of us who love the personal essay have been waiting for this book since William Bradley's wonderful essays started to appear in print about a decade ago. Now, the book is here and, like its author (upon being awakened to the joys of reading by a novelization of *Nightmare on Elm Street*), I am here to testify that "I didn't just read the book—I devoured it like a Romero zombie devours brains." Trust me, Gentle Reader, so will you. Bradley's brain will fill your brain. You will romp from the joys of Superman and *Days of Our Lives* to the joys of Flannery O'Connor, Charles Lamb and, of course, fractal founder Benoit Mandlebrot. This cultural range is fun but also necessary, for our hero must do battle with the vindictive chaplain of a Christian college, a terribly mean grandmother, and Hodgkin's lymphoma. These essays are full of enviable accomplishments but most of all they tell us a love story in which our hero finds the beloved Emily, a beautiful Renaissance scholar who is "able to talk about books and art" but who can also "appreciate the sublime genius of Don Knotts's performance in *The Ghost and Mr. Chicken*." You'll laugh, you'll cry, and you'll have spent your money well. This is a wonderful book.

Ned Stuckey-French, author of *The American Essay in The American Century*

A fierce and tender exploration of life's great paradox: that the human body can fail us, repeatedly, even in youth, but that the human heart's capacity for love and wonder at humanity is boundless. These fractal-essays, fragmented miniatures representing the whole of one man's story, shimmer like rare jewels. With keen intellect, compassion, and scalpel-sharp wit, this book succeeds where other cancer memoirs do not in illuminating the loneliness and terror of catastrophic illness while rendering unstintingly the beauty and oddness of ordinary life. A love letter to his wife, and to daytime TV, David Bowie, Don Knotts, car travel in the boonies, middle school dorkiness, Marvel comics, and the essay itself, Bradley's cumulative self-portrait illustrates Michel de Montaigne's adage that "Every man has within himself the entirety of the human condition." Funny, wise, sad, and uplifting, this collection of taut essays is a treasure-trove.

Natalia Rachel Singer, author of *Scraping by in the Big Eighties*

Fractals

William Bradley

Lavender Ink
New Orleans
lavenderink.org

∿

Fractals
by William Bradley
Copyright © 2016 by William Bradley and Lavender Ink
All rites reserved. No part of this work may be reproduced etc.

Printed in the U.S.A.
First Printing
10 9 8 7 6 5 4 3 2 1   16 17 18 19 20 21

Book design: Bill Lavender

Library of Congress Control Number: 2015949209
Bradley, William.
Fractals / William Bradley
p. cm.

ISBN: 978-1-935084-89-1 (pbk.)

Lavender Ink
New Orleans
lavenderink.org

Contents

Prologue: On Soap Operas Or The Bald and the Beautiful   15

And Never Show Thy Head by Day nor Light   21

Tina   24

How We Got Our Dog   26

Fear   30

Julio At Large   38

Cathode   41

Nana   43

ABVD PGA Champ   46

Best Thing   48

As One Might Expect   51

Marked   53

Chrononaut   59

First Thing   74

Peace Through More Power Than A Locomotive   79

What the Survey Doesn't Say   83

Dislocated   86

Life on Mars   97

Harbor Lights Coming Into View   100

The Essayist's Creed   102

Dream Child: A Reverie   111

You're a Wonder   116

Self-Similar   118

Traditional Thanksgiving Recipe   121

Ham's Lesson   125

What the Wedding Photos Don't Show   131

Epilogue: On Soap Operas
or
We Read and Watch Our Stories In Order to Live   133

Acknowledgements   143

About the Author   145

Fractals

"A cauliflower shows how an object can be made of many parts, each of which is like a whole, but smaller. Many plants are like that. A cloud is made of billows upon billows upon billows that look like clouds. As you come closer to a cloud you don't get something smooth, but irregularities at a smaller scale." (Benoit Mandelbrot)

"Every man has within himself the entirety of the human condition." (Michel de Montaigne)

Prologue: On Soap Operas Or The Bald and the Beautiful

(Columbia, Missouri, 2003)

General Hospital was particularly good today. Brenda and Jason's trial for Alcazar's murder began, but Brenda did not appear in court. They are both innocent, of course. Framed, most likely, by one of Sonny's enemies. Could be A.J. Could be Roy. It might even be that conniving Edward Quartermaine, who hates Sonny for adopting his great-grandson Michael and raising him as his own. Only one thing's certain—I'll be tuning in tomorrow.

Ostensibly, these soap operas are just on for background noise, something to fill the silence of the apartment while I write next semester's syllabuses or dust the bookshelves or make notes for my book. But as I do these things, I find my gaze wandering towards the television, where dark, chiseled men have their arms around the waists of slim, gorgeous women and say things like, "You taught me what it means to love." And I find myself ignoring the important, mundane tasks of real life, preferring, instead, a world of mobsters, secret agents, teenage lovers, and evil twins.

And later, as my fiancée and I sit on the couch, watching a documentary or a foreign film, she tells me about something she read earlier in the afternoon about the roles women played in Middleton's city comedies, and I respond with, "You know, I'm pretty sure that Cameron is Zander's father, but he doesn't realize that he's right there in Port Charles."

Emily's pretty easygoing, and she puts up with a lot of inane comments, but at this she sighs and says, "How can you watch those things?"

"They're da bomb," I answer.

She doesn't say anything as I grin at her. Just tries not to smile. In our relationship, it is generally understood that she is the serious one, and that I'm the fool she puts up with. She plays the straight man, rolling her eyes and groaning at me. Deep down, though, I think part of the reason we get along so well is that she finds me charming in my goofiness.

So I elaborate. "It's like, I like soap operas because the actors get to say things like, 'I will destroy you.'"

"Uh-huh," she says, raising her eyebrows and folding her arms across her chest. "And that appeals why?"

"Well, I mean, it's funny. How many times have you told someone you were going to destroy him?"

"Never."

"Exactly. Me neither. But they say it all the time on soap operas. 'I will destroy you.' It's awesome. I'd love to be able to say dialogue like that. Also, I like it when the guys on the shows are all dark and seductive. Like, they always look out of the tops of their eyes, really intense. Like this." I lower my head slightly and gaze at her with the most smoldering intensity I can muster. Lowering my voice, I say, "I can see the light of a thousand stars in your eyes."

"Ooookay," she says, pushing away from my chest and rising from the couch. She walks out of the room, towards the kitchen.

My mother is really the only person I can talk soap operas with. When I was sick and living with my parents, my mother and I would spend our afternoons in the living room, watching adulterers and blackmailers scheme, while the heroic characters struggled to overcome the obstacles these villains placed in front of them. And the amazing thing was, the good guys almost always did overcome. Sure, the villains might gain a temporary victory or two, and—if an actor decided to leave a show—a heroic character's plane might crash into the Pacific or something.

But the thing about soap operas—and this gets left out when people criticize them—is that virtue is always rewarded, and vice is always punished. If you cheat on your wife, she will eventually find out and leave you for your brother. If you fake your child's DNA test, the real father will eventually piece things together and raise the kid with his new, good-hearted wife. If you try to use your weather controlling device to freeze the entire town of Port Charles—and all of its citizens— in an effort to conquer the world as a power-mad dictator, the device will eventually be turned on you and you will wind up being frozen alive.

I think we can all learn a lot from that.

More importantly, though, soap operas offer a type of permanence, something you can always count on. Actors may change, super-couples may ride off into the sunset, heroic characters may eventually be replaced by younger, hotter bodies that look better shirtless or in a bikini, but you can usually turn on a soap opera—any soap opera—and figure out what's going on pretty quickly. The good guys show their teeth when they smile; the bad guys smirk. The eyes of the villainess will dart about nervously, while the heroine's gaze stays fixed and constant. Storylines may end, but they're guaranteed to reappear a few years later. One character's evil twin will be taken care of, but someone else will have a doppelganger soon enough; the popular couple will face a grave threat to their relationship, but in the end they'll emerge stronger than ever; the character who dies will come back, if he's charismatic enough to have left an impression on the viewers.

As I watched while chemotherapy devoured my cancer—and the lining of my stomach, and my hair follicles— I was struck by the feeling that some of these shows might go on forever. Many of them—*The Young and the Restless*, *Days of Our Lives*, *General Hospital*—were on long before I was born, and it was easy enough to imagine that they would continue long after I am gone.

As my condition deteriorated, my mother and I moved from the couch in the living room to the uncomfortable, sterilized furniture of the hospital room (perhaps a dying room) in Ann Arbor. And still those beautiful people appeared on the glowing box, alternately pledging eternal love and planning corporate takeovers. The shows came on everyday, predictable as predestination, while I got sicker and sicker. In that hospital room, handsome men made love to beautiful women while I vomited up tiny mouthfuls of bile—all that was left in my stomach—and felt my intestines burn with painful diarrhea, all while the tissue in my mouth cracked and fell apart. Things got worse and worse for me, until... until...

Until, at the very last moment, a crack team of medical specialists arrived to administer one last, experimental treatment. Drs. Monica and Alan Quatermaine, Dr. Rick Weber, and Nurse Bobbie Spencer arrived from Port Charles' General Hospital; Dr. John Hudson and Dr. Jamie Frame were flown in from Bay City General; Dr. Ben Davidson came all the way from Llanview, Pennsylvania. "You'll be fine," Bobbie whispered to me as the doctors tried to work a miracle. Fighting back tears, she said, "I won't let you die."

"He's coding!" Ben exclaimed.

"No," Alan shouted as he worked above me. "I won't lose this one. Not him. Not him!"

"Don't you die on me," Monica pleaded. "Don't you die on me."

And suddenly, at the last possible moment, the machinery started beeping rhythmically.

"His cancer!" Jamie exclaimed. "It's going into remission!"

"It's a miracle," John replied, clenching his jaw.

Okay. That's not exactly how it happened, but that's close enough. There wasn't actually a beeping machine, but my doctors did work diligently, and I survived as a result of their efforts.

My continued survival could indeed be considered miraculous, considering how close to cancellation The Days of *My* Life actually came.

These days, I find soap operas comforting. Cars blow up, pregnancies are faked, lies get told, and people are shot. But none of it is surprising. No one has ever watched a soap opera and said, "My God! I can't believe that happened!" I doubt anyone's life has ever been changed by something he or she saw on a daytime drama.

This, I think, is why Emily is so surprised by my fascination with these shows. We both study literature for a living, and we both believe in the transformative power of art. What's more, we both turn up our noses at movies and television shows that pander or simplify—particularly when they seem to aspire to profundity.

But I still love soap operas. They don't pretend to have any amount of depth, the way primetime dramas frequently tend to. The most they can offer is predictability, stability. And in a world where wars get launched for dubious reasons, where a college professor with multiple degrees may find his livelihood threatened by a fickle state legislature's cutbacks in education, and where a 21-year-old is forced to realize that his life can—and likely will—be snuffed out, probably without much notice, that type of stability can feel like divine intervention.

I often wish that life were more like a soap opera. It's not that I need more melodrama in my life—I had quite enough during my cancer years—but their simplified worlds seem easier to live in. For example, when my grandmother died, Emily and I had a conversation about our future, and I had to tell her—as gently as I could—that I will most likely die much sooner than she will; my medical history practically guarantees it. I will die before her; I will leave her alone. I know that this is the type of thing everyone says, but I really wanted her to understand that her happiness means everything to me, and that I didn't want her to waste her life with anger or regret if she became a young widow, as she very well could.

It was hard for us both, but it was something that had to be done. I didn't feel that we could commit till death do us part until we had discussed what exactly that could mean. I was afraid that she was unaware of the risks, that my own positive attitude and goofy charm might have given her the impression that there was nothing to be scared of, in terms of my cancer and the chances for a relapse or damage from long-term side-effects of treatment.

It turned out I needn't have worried. She tearfully assured me that she understood the risks, and the likelihood that she would go on without me someday. That getting married means that, when the relationship ends, rather than dividing up the CDs and books and movies, one person buries the other in the ground. She put her face against my chest and cried, and I reminded her that we are both in perfect health, and would likely live for a long, long time.

And I wished that life were a soap opera. I wished that, instead of sitting on the couch like that offering weak reassurances, I could lift her up in my arms, kiss her neck, chin, and lips, and tell her, with certainty, that things would always be good.

"There's never anything for you to worry about, ever again. When I'm thoughtless or cruel, it's not me; it's my evil twin. If my plane goes down, my car blows up, or for some other reason you have to order my headstone, don't despair. It's okay. I will be back, a few years later, in a dramatic, triumphant return. Love never dies, and nor will I."

But since life isn't a soap opera, I just kept my arm around her shoulders and periodically kissed the top of her head until it was time to go to sleep.

And Never Show Thy Head by Day nor Light

I t must have been spring or summer, but the seasons didn't really have too much meaning back then, before I started kindergarten and began living my life by the calendar. Some days we wore jackets; some days we wore shorts. We didn't dress ourselves back then anyway; we just wore whatever Mom picked out for us.

But as I said, it must have been spring or summer because my younger brother Steve and I were playing in the front yard, and there were bugs and birds and I recall the day being quite bright. We had a lot of energy—two boys who were five and three—and our mother would frequently shoo us out of the house so we could run around and exhaust ourselves without smashing anything inside.

We were taking a break from playing, sitting by the tree near the driveway, when one of the bugs caught my eye. It was on the ground, black and yellow striped, legs flailing in the air helplessly. Years later, when I would read Virginia Woolf, her own moth reminded me of this creature. I think I was aware, even then, that the bug was dying. I thought maybe we could help, though I wasn't too sure about touching a strange bug myself

"Look," I said, pointing to the ground. Steve crouched in to get a closer glance.

"What is it?" he asked.

"A caterpillar," I told him.

"What's he doing on his back?"

"He's stuck." I looked at my brother. "Roll him over."

He reached out and touched the bug, then screamed and began to cry.

"It hurts!" he wailed.

My mother was there, lifting him up, faster than could be believed.

"What happened?" she asked as she carried him inside and I trailed behind her. "What happened?"

"He touched a bug," I said. "Then he started crying."

She sat him on the kitchen counter and examined his fingers.

"Okay," she said to me. "Go across the street—look both ways—and ask Mrs. Zuckerman if she knows what to do when a little boy gets stung by a wasp."

I didn't know what a wasp was, of course, but I remembered what my mom said, and Mrs. Zuckerman—my mom's best friend, our occasional babysitter—walked me back over to our house with a box of baking soda. I assume my mom realized that, most often, wasp stings aren't fatal. But neither of us had ever been stung before, and perhaps she thought wasp venom might be deadly for someone so small. Or, perhaps, she panicked upon hearing her three-year-old's agonized screams.

Older siblings often inflict pain on their younger siblings. Sometimes accidentally, other times with more malice. In the years to come, I would make fun of Steve for being held back in the first grade. I would yell at him to stop following my friends and me around. I would go skinny dipping with his girlfriend. I would call him a fag, not realizing—unless I actually did, because I might have—that he was actually gay. I would accuse him of being melodramatic when he expressed his anxiety about coming completely out of the closet. I would date a fundamentalist Christian who he insisted would look at him with revulsion. Well into our twenties, I would refuse to speak to him for months at a time.

I don't think he has ever told on me, though at times he could have gotten me into well-deserved trouble. He certainly never told my mother why he reached out and touched a wasp, who encouraged him to do such a thing. And though we get along quite well now that we're in our mid-thirties and can see middle age on the horizon, I can't help but feel like something of a restless wanderer of the earth, marked by the guilt I feel over having failed to be my brother's keeper.

Tina

Though recess was usually devoted to dodge ball, freeze tag, or trying to breakdance, on some days the temperature just climbed too high, and my friends—Marco, Byron, Billy—and I would just hang out by the school building, enjoying what little shade the structure offered. We'd stand, backs against the wall, talking about Ghostbusters or Duran Duran or Q-Bert or whatever else we were into that day. Hands in the pockets of our Jams shorts, slouching, looking tough. Had we been any older, we probably would have smoked. As it was, we were content to look as bad-ass as we could, for third-graders.

Girls did not hang around with our group. They played four-square while we played dodgeball, and if it was too hot to play, then they would congregate in their own groups, talking and giggling. Contrary to stereotypes and expectations, we did not have an antagonistic relationship with the girls. We were simply indifferent, and the available evidence indicated that they felt the same about us.

On one particular hot day, though, as my friends and I debated over something like whether Turbo Teen would win in a race against KITT, from *Knight Rider*, a line was crossed. Tina, from my class, approached our group, and stared at me. I tried not to look at her—for the first time, making eye contact with a girl was suddenly very difficult as she just stood there, like she was waiting for something. And when I finally glanced in her direction, she smiled. She was missing one of her front teeth.

"I love you, Billy" she said. "You and Magnum P.I. If Magnum won't marry me, I want to marry you. When we grow up."

I stared at her for a moment, then turned to my friends. They were looking at me, apparently as surprised as I was. It was obvious that they didn't know the proper response either.

I looked back at her. "Okay," I said. It occurred to me that I should probably say, "I love you too," because, even though I hadn't thought of it before, it seemed to be true at the moment—and besides, wasn't it what she was expecting?

So I said it. "I love you too." She grinned again, and for some reason, I felt myself returning her smile.

"Okay. See you later then." And she was gone, back to her own crowd. I turned to my friends, and our conversation about whatever it was we talked about slowly got back on track.

Tina and I never spoke to each other again—apparently, Tom Selleck would have her after all. Good for her, I suppose; though I would later own a collection of Hawaiian shirts, I have never driven a convertible. Couldn't even grow a decent mustache until well after college. Really, when all is said and done, it's better this way, for both of us. And yet, years later, the memory of this moment from the third grade would occur to me from time to time—usually after a bad break-up—and I would have to admit that, when all was said and done, this brief conversation represented the least complicated relationship I would ever be in.

Even if I had to share her affections with Magnum.

How We Got Our Dog

My one daily chore, when I was seven, was to fetch the newspaper from the front yard. *The Sacramento Bee*. My father was—and still is—a newspaper publisher, but his paper—*The Willows Journal*—wasn't a daily, and wasn't delivered in the mornings. So he would read the Sacramento paper while he ate his Cheerios and drank his coffee. I didn't really think of it as a chore, though—in fact, I liked doing this. I didn't need to be asked, and my father always said "Thank you" when I brought the paper to him, and it brought me happiness to know that I had pleased him. I loved my dad, and I loved that he loved me.

On one particular morning I ran from the front door into the yard, squishing the dew-covered grass under my small, bare feet. I would run to the newspaper, grab it without stopping, then turn around and run back to the house, fast as I could. Like I did every day. I liked to imagine that I was young Clark Kent in the *Superman* movie, outrunning the train as it passed through the fields of Smallville.

As I was running back to the house, I noticed that something seemed different. I stopped and stared. The house *was* different—there were strange designs all over it, designs that I had never seen before. The house—which my parents had built—was a Southwestern style, pueblo sort of dwelling. "You don't paint this type of house," my father had told us as the house was being constructed. Yet someone had painted it. Or at least painted on it. These designs appeared all over the front of the house, from the garage on one side all the way to the wall by my bedroom window on the other side—whoever had done this must have gotten onto the porch.

I walked into the kitchen. My father smiled at me and held his hand out for the paper.

"I need to show you something," I told him.

Standing on the lawn, his shoulders slumped, my father shook his head and muttered, "Aw, no." Then he went inside to get my mom to show her.

They had even painted one of these designs on the hood of my father's car.

"It's called a swastika," my mother told us as we sat at the kitchen table while my dad talked to the police. Because my mom sometimes speaks with a New England accent, I wasn't sure if she was saying swastika or swasticker. I made a mental note to ask my dad what it was called. "It's a symbol of people who did horrible, horrible things to Jewish people. It's a terrible, nasty symbol."

"But we're Catholic," my brother pointed out. "Why paint a symbol about Jews on our house?"

My mother didn't have an answer.

Later that day, my mom picked us up from school and we drove to the newspaper office to pick up Dad, who had to be driven to the car dealership, where they were removing the offensive symbol from his car. Then, we would all go home—my brother and sister stayed in the station wagon with Mom, but I got out of the car with my dad. I wanted to ride home with him.

Inside the dealership, a man I'd never met before shook my father's hand and put a reassuring hand on his shoulder. "It's just disgusting," he said. "Awful."

"Thanks," my dad replied, taking out his checkbook.

"There's no charge," the man said. "I'm happy to do this for you."

My dad tried to protest, but the man wouldn't hear of it. "You're a good man, Joe. This shouldn't have happened to you."

My dad thanked him, and we walked out to the car. Dad didn't put his seatbelt on right away, though. "Wait here," he said as he got out of the car. He returned a moment later. "I couldn't convince him to take any money," he would tell my mom later.

From time to time, I've wondered about the man who painted the swastikas on our house nearly three decades ago. At first, I was frightened by the idea that he had been right outside my bedroom window, that he might have even seen me, fast asleep. I thought that I was lucky he didn't decide to murder me—all crimes were the same, as far as I was concerned back then. I never learned the man's name, but I do know that he was someone who had worked for my dad, who my dad had fired. I think perhaps the man had stolen money or equipment, maybe to support a drug problem, but sometimes I think I just made up that detail when I was a kid in order to explain why my dad would fire somebody and cause so much anger and hatred. The Dad I knew liked to tell jokes and play Pac Man and teach us how to throw a spiral. I couldn't imagine someone hating him. But someone did—he seemed to think he knew my dad in a way that I did not. My brother and I didn't understand it at the time, but the vandal wasn't trying to use the swastika to intimidate us—he was calling my father a Nazi. And he must have felt justified—he bought spray paint, drove out to our house in the dead of night, crept around the yard, up on the porch, and certainly must have seen the second grader asleep in his bed beside the window while he left his mark. Did he reconsider when he saw me? Did he delight in the idea that my parents would have to explain what had happened, what he had done, to their kids? Did he feel sorry for me, believing that I was an innocent child being raised by a fascist? Did he hate me too? Does he ever think about me now, 29 years later, the way I still think about him from time to time?

My parents were apparently frightened by the idea of a stranger coming up on the porch and peering in on us while we slept too, though, because a few weeks later we got a big dog – a

German shorthair, who spent every night at the foot of my bed for the rest of my childhood.

Fear

My wife and I each paid $20 to attend the one-night-only 25th anniversary screening of the original *A Nightmare on Elm Street* several years ago. This was at a point in our marriage where we probably couldn't afford to blow $40 on a movie, but I had just started my first academic job and, for the first time, we had an annual household income of over $25,000, so we felt rich. And more importantly, I love *A Nightmare on Elm Street*, and was excited for the opportunity to see it on the big screen.

If you asked me for my favorite horror movie, I would honestly tell you that it's *The Shining*. Kubrick's use of tracking shots, Bela Bartok's score, Shelly Duvall's performance as an abused woman trying to survive in an icy, opulent hell— it's all amazing, and remains unnerving every time I watch it. But if I have a few beers tonight and decide I want to watch a scary movie, I'll probably put something like *Friday the 13th Part 3* in the DVD player. You can watch it in 3D in the comfort of your own home, you know. But more importantly, I find that cheesy slasher movies from the 70s and 80s just have their own sort of goofy charm. Yes, they're violent, and more than a little misogynist. But it's so hard for me to take them seriously at this point. Even though they were rated "R," they seem, in their simple-minded black-and-white morality, childish to me. Not of the morally-complicated adult world I live in, that's for sure. So watching movies like these reminds me of my childhood, keeps me tethered to the dorky, horror-obsessed kid I was, and—I sometimes like to imagine—in some ways keeps me young.

Even before I saw my first horror movie, I found them fascinating. When I was a kid, my parents were diligent in shielding us from movie gore and anything remotely scary; the idea, I know, was to protect our impressionable minds from anything that might upset or disturb us, but I'm afraid it didn't entirely work. In fact, as I got closer to my middle school years and realized most of my friends had seen *Halloween* and *Silent Night, Deadly Night*, I became acutely aware that my parents had been sheltering me, that there was a whole world of supernaturally-powerful serial killers and blood-thirsty demons out there. And though I understood, rationally, that these things only existed in movies, on some level I think I perceived something menacing about the adult world as a result of my parents' zealous protection. After all, if there were nothing to really be afraid of, then why would I need to be protected?

But maybe that's not quite right. Maybe my brother and I detected menace before becoming aware of these movies, and that's what caused my parents to try to shield us from multiplex mayhem. I know that the witch in the *Wizard of Oz* scared me when I was a kid; so too did Dr. Banner's transformation into *The Incredible Hulk* on TV. And my brother couldn't stand to be in the room when *The Electric Company* started—the voice that yelled "Hey You Guys!" would cause him to cry if he heard it. And, truth be told, he was well into adulthood before he could force himself to watch the scene in *Indiana Jones and the Temple of Doom* where the villain rips the guy's heart out of his chest. So, perhaps my parents—realizing that their sons were high-strung and easily frightened—understood that they had to be on their toes when it came to shielding us from big-screen frights.

Or, maybe I'm over-thinking the whole thing, and responsible parents just don't let their kids watch R-rated movies full of naked breasts and chainsaw-wielding madmen who want to turn teenagers into barbecue sandwiches.

The bottom line is, by the time I was in the fifth grade, most of my friends had seen at least some of these movies, and I had not. I was fascinated by the very idea of these forbidden movies, what they said about the adult world, and why my parents felt the need to shield me even while my friends' parents did not feel a similar need to shield them. Plus, there was that nagging suspicion—then, as adolescence was just on the horizon—that there was something more than a little lame about not knowing anything about these movies that were so important to my classmates. I was already beginning to understand that I was a dork—a label that would stay with me at least through the beginning of high school—and part of that dorkiness came, I understood, from my naïveté when it came to these elements of the popular culture that were so important to kids in the eighties.

I found my entrance into this world of horror that my friends knew so well one morning in the cafeteria before the first bell rang to send us to our classrooms. A kid I knew, Jeremy Tenney, had a book in front of him—*The Nightmares on Elm Street*, the official novelization of the first three Freddy Krueger movies. The films' logo—which looked like it had been scribbled by a madman with a nerve disorder—was splashed across the cover, with Freddy's razor-fingered glove hanging down, blades partially obscuring the title with the blood that dripped from them.

In all of my eleven years, I had never seen a book that looked so cool.

"Good book?" I asked him.

He nodded. "Yeah. The movies are better, though."

Of course they were, I thought. "Why are you reading the book then?"

He shrugged. "I just really liked the movies." I think he must have intuited my interest, because he said, "I'm almost done with it. I'll bring it tomorrow, if you want to borrow it."

Jackpot. Jeremy had allowed me to find a loophole in my parents' "No Horror Movie" rule. They didn't make R-rated books, after all—and weren't my parents always on my case about reading anyway? Even if they found the book, I could always use their previously-articulated arguments in favor of literacy against them. Finally, I had won. I would learn exactly what was so scary that my parents had felt the need to protect me.

I felt certain that reading the *Nightmare on Elm Street* book would allow me a deeper understanding of the real world.

I didn't just read the book—I devoured it like a Romero zombie devours brains.

As I read it, I realized that books, too, could be scary. I had an imagination vivid enough to picture what it must have been like for Rod to see Tina's sleeping body rudely lifted from the bed by an invisible force, shoved to the ceiling and split open by unseen razor fingers. I could see Tina running from Freddy, his arms somehow long enough to stretch across the entire alley, affording her no escape. I could imagine Jesse's dread as he came to realize that Freddy intended to possess his body in order to kill in the waking world.

The irony is, I probably would have been better off watching the movies, as far as my own fear went. When I finally saw the movies I did find them scary, but I also realized that Rod and Tina were obnoxious and older than they should have been— they spoke the way people in their thirties think teenagers speak ("I woke up with a hard-on that had your name on it." "Tina's a four-letter word—your joint's not big enough for four letters."). The scene where Freddy chases Tina down the alley looks so fake it made me giggle when I finally saw it for the first time. And Jesse was just an irritating whiner—if Freddy wants him so badly, let him have him, I'd later say.

But that's not how I responded to the novelizations. No, the novelizations were simply terrifying, and—since Freddy Krueger killed kids in their sleep—I promptly resolved to never sleep again.

I didn't actually make the decision consciously, of course. I may have had an overactive imagination and very little idea about how the real world worked, but I wasn't an absolute moron. I knew, logically, that child murderers do not come back from the dead to haunt the dreams of the children whose parents burned them alive in their own boiler rooms. It just didn't happen—and if it had, it would have been all over the news. No, if people could come back from the dead and hang out in people's dreams, I was fairly certain that my grandfather would have checked in from time-to-time. The premise of the movies was not grounded in reality—it all came from this guy, Wes Craven, who wrote and directed the first movie. And, I could convince myself during the day, that guy probably lived in a mansion in Hollywood, surrounded by movie stars and supermodels, and hardly ever thought about this creation of his that was haunting me so.

That was my rational mind. But how many perfectly rational 11-year-olds do you know—particularly when they're in a dark room and the rest of the family is asleep and the house is making weird noises?

My parents realized pretty quickly that I seemed groggier than usual at breakfast, and that I was falling asleep while watching TV in the afternoon. And I eventually had to tell them that I wasn't sleeping much at night anymore, and why. I can't say my parents were angry with me, but nor were they particularly pleased. When all is said and done, I think the situation kind of annoyed them. "You're not sleeping because you're afraid that a boogeyman in a fedora hat that you read about in the adaptation to a movie you've never seen is going to kill you?" I don't think that's the type of question any father wants to ask his son.

As stupid as they surely found the situation, I have to say that my parents bent over backwards to help me to sleep again. No more drifting off in the afternoons. A big glass of warm milk before bed. God love them, at one point they even took me to our family doctor, apparently hoping that there was a pill or something that would make me forget to be such a neurotic coward. The doctor, for his part, seemed confused about what his role in this personal drama was supposed to be. "I would say," he eventually concluded, "he needs to get over it and start sleeping again."

Which is exactly what happened. As time passed, my terror over what I'd read faded. In a few weeks, it all seemed silly, and I was quite embarrassed by the whole episode. Scared by a movie character? How lame. I promised myself that I would never mistake supernatural fiction for reality ever again.

I kept that promise, too. For several months. Until the USA Network showed *Children of the Corn* one afternoon when I was home sick, and the process repeated itself. Just as it would a year or so later when I saw *Halloween* for the first time. And then again with *Friday the 13th*. These movies terrified me, when I was a kid, but I couldn't stay away from them.

As an adult, it's a rare and special thing to find a horror movie that's genuinely scary. *The Shining*, *The Exorcist*, and *Alien* still retain the ability to unnerve, and I'll occasionally find an older movie, like Bob Clark's original *Black Christmas*, that really freaks me out. But too much of what passes for horror these days seems watered-down, or too outlandishly dumb to be taken seriously, or just not scary. I can't imagine anyone watching the recent *A Nightmare on Elm Street* remake and actually getting frightened.

Of course, part of the problem is, I've found new things to be scared of. As it happens, my parents were shielding me from the menacing adult world; it was just the nature of the menace that I'd misunderstood. There are no doll serial killers or leather fetishist demons with pins in their heads—instead, there are religious extremists with bombs. There are factories dumping carcinogens into streams. There are people who think a life devoted to literature and art is simply decadent. There's waterboarding.

I fear that my writing is mediocre at best. I fear that my wife no longer finds me as physically attractive as she used to. I fear that I'll never realize my dream of becoming a tenured professor. I fear impotence. School shootings. Stand your ground laws. Getting drunk and revealing how offensive and obnoxious my internal monologue actually is. Cancer. Being revealed as the academic and artistic fraud I'm pretty sure I am. That my parents will die. That my wife will decide she no longer loves me.

These are the things that terrify me. Sometimes, the only way to calm my nerves and quell the fear is to turn my brain off and watch a madman with a butcher's knife stalk and then kill some babysitters.

The 25th anniversary screening of *A Nightmare on Elm Street* was kind of a bust, actually. I had this idea that the theater would be filled with aging Gen-Xers excited to recapture the experience of being a child of the 1980s again. And there were a few of us like that in the audience. But there was also a group of about fifteen teenagers sitting down in front, and they were pretty rowdy—shouting things at the screen, giggling, running around the theater, making and receiving phone calls. My shushing got louder as the movie went on; a woman roughly my age sitting nearby eventually shouted at the kids, "Shut the fuck up!"

"This is ridiculous," I kept whispering to my wife.

"Do you want to go complain?" was her constant reply.

I didn't. I didn't want to be the type of person who gets annoyed with young people. I didn't want to be someone who gets angry at the sound of teenagers laughing. I hated the idea that I was the type of grumpy old man who said things like "Get off my lawn!" or who had groups of teenagers thrown out of places because of shenanigans and tomfoolery.

Towards the end of the movie, as Nancy is setting her traps for Freddy, one of the teenage girls came walking up the aisle, gabbing into her phone.

"Oh I know," she said, "it's soooooo stupid, but funny…"

As she walked past me, I leaned towards the aisle and shushed her as loud as I could.

She stopped and adjusted the phone so that it wasn't near her mouth. I was expecting her to whisper "Sorry," but instead she looked right at me and shouted, "Shut up!"

I was shocked, startled both by her viciousness and the phrase that entered my head immediately: "My God, I would never have spoken that way to an adult when I was her age."

When I was her age. Back in the day. The good old days? The grown-ups I knew when I was a kid didn't think so—they thought we were out of control, with crack cocaine, gangs, drive-by shootings, teen pregnancy, and N.W.A. Of course, their parents thought they were out of control, with their LSD, free love, campus protests, left-wing radicals, and The Beatles.

Unexpectedly, I did experience fear that night—the fear that comes from knowing that, somewhere along the line, you became old without realizing it, and you'll never know the reckless energy of youth again.

Julio At Large

I hadn't known the girl very well, and rarely gave her much thought before she disappeared the summer between ninth and tenth grade. We both had last names that started with the letter "B," so we frequently had to sit next to each other in classes where our teachers couldn't be bothered to come up with a creative way to assign seats. I didn't particularly like her, but I didn't dislike her either— she was just kind of there.

Until she wasn't. One day, my dad came home at lunch with the newspaper—fresh off the press— in his hand. "Do you know this girl?" She looked more interesting in black and white. "She's missing," he said. "Her parents think she was kidnapped." I guess everyone's parents were frightened for a couple of days, although even the early articles included quotes from the police chief saying that—her parents' certainty aside—there was no evidence to suggest she was taken against her will.

People seemed to think that she would be found somewhere in town, which meant we were all surprised two weeks later to learn that she and her companion—a local boy who hadn't even been reported missing— had been charged with indecent exposure on a beach in Florida. Of course he was older than she was—old enough to drive, not old enough for it to be a felony.

My dad was disgusted by both the immorality and stupidity of it all. "They would have gotten away," he said, "if they'd managed to keep their clothes on." Her mother, of course, was mortified. She'd come down to the newspaper office the day before to try to convince my father not to publish the truth—a wasted effort, as they'd been covering the story for weeks and had already devoted several column inches to the family's kidnapping theory. My father's insistence that he had an obligation fell on deaf ears, though. "It's not her fault," the mother said. "He seduced her; he made it sound so romantic, like… Romeo and Julio." The second name she pronounced "jew-lee-oh," which made both my mother and me laugh when my dad told us.

But even if I shared my parents' opinion that the mother was dumb, I couldn't bring myself to believe that the girl herself was a victim of her own stupidity. Oh, I agreed with my father out loud, but in my heart of hearts I knew that this quiet, bored girl I'd never really thought about before was now the bravest and coolest person I'd ever met. Because I knew what she knew, and what our parents had forgotten: when you're fifteen, the world tries to crush you. Teachers, parents, cops—the only escape from their tedious gaze came in the form of heavy metal videos and the occasional party with friends who felt similarly suffocated. Life sucked, it was all bullshit, and any relief to be found was only temporary. Then, it was back to the world of chores and standardized tests.

But not for her. Not for a couple of weeks, anyway. She did what the rest of us were afraid to do. Made it all the way from our dreary coal mining town to a place of tropical opulence, with no one assigning her a book to read or forcing her to take the garbage out the entire time. It was just freedom, with the boy she loved by her side (and on top of her and underneath her and behind her, the fearful virgin that I was imagined). And yeah, she got caught. But didn't she have to? True, she and her guy didn't hurt people, the way Bonnie and Clyde and Mickey and Mallory and other famously unconventional couples did, but it seems to me that no one who declares "me and you against the world" honestly believes he or she is going to win—that's why so few do it. Her story could have ended with prostitution, or a violent break-up, or just the call to home from a truck stop—"Mom, come get me." But instead, I liked to think, Julio took charge of her situation— walked into the surf, removed her bikini bottoms, and wrapped her legs around the boy who did not kidnap her, saying "fuck

me" to him and "fuck you" to the world of the oppressive and
the oppressed as it looked on, terrified and scandalized, from the
safety of the beach.

Cathode

S ometimes, my memory is like an old television set, turned on after the show has started. The screen takes a few minutes to warm up, the picture coming into view as a cathode ray tube writes analog signals, showing us—finally—a chubby kid standing on a sidewalk. The camera captures him from above, through a dirty second-story window. Pan left, there's Rob, staring down at him. Pan right, there's Pat, slack-jawed. Down below, the kid is glaring at his observers. Even from a distance, they can tell he's trying not to cry. He extends both arms away from his body, then extends both middle fingers, then continues to storm down the street.

He had invited all of us over the night before. He wanted us to camp out in his backyard and play *Dungeons and Dragons* or *Marvel Superheroes* all night, which is something we frequently did in the woods near my house, but never out at his home. None of us really liked going over to Mike's, which was always messy and drafty, way out in the West Virginia wilderness. His parents were strange. His dad was frequently gone, and his mom—a teacher at the middle school we'd all just graduated from—seemed to spend most of her time screaming at her younger children.

I don't know which of us mentioned it first, that day as our role-playing game club met in the office above the bookstore where we bought our ten-sided dice. But gradually, we realized that none of us—and we numbered over half a dozen, I'm sure—had gone out to the house in the woods. Nobody even bothered to call to decline the invitation. We laughed about this, and I guess we laughed when he flipped us off, too, although that was a more nervous laughter, a way to reassure ourselves that we hadn't done anything wrong. He was just being a wuss.

Later that afternoon, at my house, we gathered our camping supplies and character sheets, ready to head out to the woods. My old TV was tuned in to the local news. This seems odd, in hindsight— 15-year-olds watching the local news? Maybe we'd been watching something else beforehand. Regardless. The top story—local middle school teacher arrested that morning for having sex with a 13-year-old student. She would later insist that he had seduced her, that she fell in love while trying to help him do better in his classes, and I don't know. Maybe. I can't really say what goes on in some people's heads, and her son never spoke to any of us again—his dad moved them away pretty quickly. All I've got is that image—the kid standing on the sidewalk, trying not to cry as he flips off the kids who were supposed to be his friends on what, I'm sure, must have been the worst day of his life. And then the image on the screen fades and caves in on itself, leaving only blankness.

Nana

I had promised my mother I wouldn't write an essay about her mother until the old lady died. More specifically, when my mother found out I was writing about the experience of having cancer when I was in my early twenties, she made me promise that I would not reveal to the world that my grandmother had once, over a breakfast of coffee and English muffins, wished out loud that I would die in order to teach my mother a lesson about grief.

My grandmother died in 2006, so I can write about her now. I have kept my promise to my mother. Yet I find that I can't write about her now after all. Or, at least, I can't tell the whole story. I can tell you that she lost her oldest son, my Uncle Billy, when he was in his thirties. I can tell you that he drowned at New Hampshire's Seabrook Beach, saving a group of children—including his own—who had been snatched by an undertow. I can tell you she was never the same after that loss—or, at least, people tell me she was never the same. That her grief created an anger directed towards the God who took her son as well as towards her other grown children, whom He had spared. I can tell you about that breakfast with my mother and her, fifteen years later, when she tearfully spat out, "You don't know what it's like to lose your son. But I hope you do someday."

But if I tell you she was never the same after the death of her son, my uncle, I think I might be suggesting something untrue. In our family lore, it was Billy's death that drove her over the edge, but there are also stories—overheard when the grown-ups thought we were asleep—that call this account into question. Had she really grabbed my grandfather's crutch and bashed him in the side with it, dislocating his recently-replaced hip, a year before Billy's death? Were my mother and uncles forced to hide under the dining room table as children while she screamed and broke plates until my grandfather could subdue her and take her to a hospital that she didn't leave for several weeks? Had my grandfather distracted his kids with a vacation to Washington, D.C. while their mother was "getting well?"

I have heard these stories—or, to be more precise, I *think* I have heard allusions to these stories—over the years. But I suspect my understanding of my family's history is corrupted by my own imagination—that I have fleshed-out these references and whispered anecdotes into fully-developed stories that exist not in history, but only in my mind. I think I know that my grandmother and grandfather found his father's dead body—a suicide—and that my grandfather never spoke of this event for the rest of his life, forbidding her to speak of it in his presence too. I think my Uncle Mike told me this, but I also think the writer in me might have invented certain details in order to provide his antiheroine with a clear and understandable motivation to, decades later, pick up the crutch and wield it against the husband who would not allow her to speak of her trauma.

I do remember that I did not like my grandmother, when I was very little. Even before Billy died. I loved my grandfather, but I remember feeling like my grandmother was mean. One of my earliest memories involves my mom sitting down with me on the couch, putting her arm around me, and telling me that I had to be nice to my grandmother. That my grandmother loved me. But I also remember realizing that my mom wasn't chastising me for anything I had said or done. I must have been around four at this point, but I remember that my mom was asking me to be nice to my grandmother as a favor to her. So I said I would. And I was. For the rest of my life, I sat silently as my grandmother berated my mother, shouted about how God had abandoned her, and wished for my death while I spread raspberry preserves over my muffin.

My mother and I do not have a particularly emotive relationship. We mostly communicate through sarcasm. My other siblings and my father are more sincere, more inclined to end a phone call with "I love you" or give a spontaneous hug. When my mother began to cry at my wedding, I glared at her and stage-whispered, "For the love of God, pull yourself together" to make her laugh.

But I think my mother and I understand each other in a way that my other family members don't understand us. And I think, now, it might have begun with that conversation 34 years ago, when we became co-conspirators in an attempt to make visits with my grandmother more tolerable. Keep our tempers in check. Turn the other cheek. Ignore the meanness. We would make things better by pretending that things *were* better.

This is why I can't ask my mother for more information about my grandmother—information I could use in writing the essay about this abusive, troubled, tragic woman. To ask my mother to go back to her own childhood and young adulthood, to explain her tormentor to me, is too much to ask. I promised not to dwell on my grandmother's cruelty, to let this stuff go. So I haven't written an essay about my grandmother.

ABVD PGA Champ

T he saline flush is slowly dripping through the plastic tube and into my veins. Pam, the head nurse, has just finished administering the last drug in my ABVD chemotherapy treatment, the DTIC-Dome. The drugs have left me feeling weary, with a heavy head and outraged, tumultuous stomach. I'm having a hard time staying awake. My head keeps falling forward, and I keep snapping back, blinking quickly, to complete consciousness. I do not want to fall asleep here. I'm afraid that if I move too suddenly, I'll accidentally tear the needle out of my arm and splash my blood on their cool white tile. This has only happened to me once, but once was enough.

There is one other patient in the sterile, fluorescent-lit chemotherapy room. He is, most likely, in his mid-sixties. Like me, he's sitting in one of the blue Barcaloungers, watching his own bag of saline empty into his body. We receive the same drug regimen, and they started us at around the same time today.

He is hooked up to an oxygen tank that is delivering air too fast, causing him to burp sporadically, which, in turn, encourages my own nausea. He has peeling radiation burns on his neck and the bottom part of his face. His wife—overweight, bad perm, denim jacket—is sitting next to him. They're keeping their own counsel, and in the course of their conversation, he periodically says things like, "I used to like living there, until those lesbos moved in across the street."

ESPN is on the television. No one watches it. I'm struggling to remain conscious, and he's looking at his wife through thick, ugly glasses that came, undoubtedly, from the $19.99 rack at the Wal-Mart optical center. "They ought to throw that lying asshole out of office once and for all," he says, punctuating his sentence with a belch. His Green Bay Packers hat does not conceal the fact that what is left of his hair is sparse and wispy. My own hair has thinned, but has not fallen out completely. I've vowed to shave my head if it gets any thinner. Feeling like shit doesn't mean you have to look like shit. Or be a shit.

He has stopped talking. Good. Something on television appeals to him at this moment. I open my eyes, see that he's watching a golf tournament, and then close them again. Is it the Master's already? Time flies.

"There's that Nigger Woods," he says in a voice thick with an Upper Michigan accent and hoarse from radiation-induced irritation.

At this, I open my eyes again. There's a limit to how much I'm willing to take; eventually you have to take a stand, even when you can't force yourself out of your blue Barcalounger. I lean forward, exhausted and weak but ready to tear into the fascist cretin. I have my liberalism, my compassion, and my intelligence working for me. And what does he have? An eighth-grade education and a lifetime in the mines, if he's lucky. I would win this argument. I understand things.

But before I can even open my mouth to respond, he turns to his wife, eyes large behind those horrible glasses. "I hope I live," he says. "I'd like to learn how to play golf too."

His wife smiles at him, sadly, and puts her hand on top of his. He grips it with his thumb and two of his fingers, looking at her for a moment before looking back at the television. I lean back in my chair and close my eyes, wordless.

Best Thing

The worst part of having cancer when you're young—at least, if you're anything like me—is not fearing death. Even if, like me, you've been aware of and troubled by your own mortality since you were a child, you don't really believe that this is the end. Because young people—even thanatophobic young people—still feel, deep down, that nothing can truly hurt them.

The worst part of having cancer when you're young isn't really the nausea and the vomiting. Yes, chemotherapy makes you sick, and no, the anti-nausea drugs—at least the ones they gave me—don't seem to help much. But young people do things like follow 12 Milwaukee's Bests with three shots of tequila and a mescal worm. Nausea and vomiting is part of the experience of being young.

The worst part of having cancer when you're young isn't losing your hair—at least, not if you're a guy like me. Look at all the cool bald guys out there—Michael Jordan, Michael Stipe, Billy Corgan, Bruce Willis, Patrick Stewart, LL Cool J. Now, not having eyebrows is weird, but you can pretty effectively cover that up by wearing your glasses all the time.

The worst part of having cancer when you're young isn't the loneliness—although, honestly, for me, that was close to the worst thing. But you can take this time to watch movies you'd always meant to see—*Rosemary's Baby*, perhaps, or *Casablanca*. You can spend your days reading comic books, getting up-to-speed on characters you used to enjoy—like Batman or Spider-Man—but had given up because the pressures of college didn't leave you much time for such diversions. And, of course, there's

Internet porn and masturbation for a temporary break from the tedium. Now make no mistake, this is boring, and it's isolating, and it leaves you feeling kind of pathetic, but it's not the worst thing.

The worst thing about having cancer when you're young—if your experience is anything like mine—is knowing that the world is moving on without you. Even as you're in a chemotherapy room, or in a hospital bed, or just confined to your parents' house, you know that your friends are applying for jobs, are getting engaged, are selling off their dorm fridges in order to put that money towards the security deposit on a small apartment. You can hear it in their voices when they call you— that nervous excitement that comes with finishing school and embarking on an unknown but thrilling future. And you know that you're stuck. That's the worst fucking thing. That feeling like everyone else is sprinting through the meadow, but you're caught in quicksand. They're getting farther and farther away from where you are, and you're sinking, and though their glances when they look back show concern, they can't stop to help you. Not for a lack of compassion—it's just not possible.

And so you feel alone, forsaken, forgotten.

But then, sometimes, someone is able to help in some small way. Your best friend's life is continuing, of course, but he makes the long drive to visit you before your bone marrow transplant, to reassure you that you're not alone.

"You're my best friend, Rad Brad," he'll say as you both stare into your beers, avoiding eye contact because when you're young and you're male and you're straight and you have cancer, you're still self-conscious about looking gay. As if that actually mattered.

"You're my best friend too," you'll tell him.

"And," he says, "you know, I love you."

"I love you too," you'll say, still avoiding eye contact, because, you know.

And then, one of you will say something vaguely homophobic even though neither of you are homophobes, and, in the years to come, you'll be embarrassed to have ever been the type of guy who made such jokes, even ironically. But this is that night, one night in 1998 when you're 22 and he's 21, and the solemnity of the moment needs to end. So you say, "Okay, Nancy, now let's go wax your vagina" or he says "Easy there, Liberace" and you'll laugh and keep drinking, talking about comic books and music and movies and other light fare. But at the end of the night, you'll hug each other anyway. And if it can be said that there is a "best thing" about having cancer when you're young, that would be it.

As One Might Expect

The nun came in the afternoon. At least, I think she was a nun. She was a small, dark-skinned, soft-spoken woman with a thick accent—something Central American or perhaps Eastern European. Although she didn't wear a habit, she had Rosary beads, and a tiny plastic statue of the Virgin Mary that she gave to me. And I could understand her question, pronounced softly in that unidentifiable accent, asked that first day, "Would you like me to pray with you?" Silly question to ask a 22-year-old guy in a hospital bed, with tubes sticking in his chest, a guy without energy, motivation, or hair. Groggy, confused, with a sense that things had been better, could be better again. Did I want to pray?

My mother was sitting in the chair off to the side of the bed, looking up from her book, watching me from behind her bifocals. That could be a reason to decline prayer. My mother had never, so far as I could remember, forced religion on us. My father would insist on going to Midnight Mass, on saying Grace, on rubbing water sent by relatives who had visited Lourdes on the lump that I'd found in my neck. My mother did not really seem to share these metaphysical concerns.

My mother was an English teacher, though, and, like me, was an avid reader. In the mystery novels she read in her spare time, my mother appreciated more than anything else a suspenseful plot, full of twists and surprises, with characters who confounded her expectations. I just liked ironic detachment in my narratives, with characters who were clever and cool and never uttered banalities. More than anything, though, my mother and I both hated clichés. And really, what could be more clichéd than the cancer patient finding God? The smug "Cathnostic" who flirted with atheism learning humility and begging to be saved?

Promising to be a better person, "if only this nightmare would end once and for all"?

Ridiculous. Horrible. More contrived than the conflicts on the soap operas we watched every day. To be so predictable, a stock character, as boring as an Amy Grant record being played at Kathy Lee Gifford's house, could be a fate worse than death, I imagined.

Could be.

But probably not.

Because perhaps most importantly, I knew at that moment, was that I was not an atheist at all. And though I knew it weakened the integrity of my narrative, introduced the clichéd into the story I'd written from myself, I realized that, in fact, I did want this nun to talk to me, to care for me, and to pray for me. I didn't know what I believed entirely, but I hoped, at the very least, that accepting her offer might deliver some type of grace.

My mother didn't say anything, just returned her focus to the novel in front of her, as I sat up from under the hospital bed's thin white sheets and let the nun—probably, she was a nun—take my hands. She closed her eyes; I closed mine as well. And the words she spoke were low, and in that heavy accent, but I made out the relevant parts. Prayers mostly tend to sound alike, after all.

Marked

"These tattoos provide a very positive tool in the treatment of cancer. During treatment they are necessary so the radiation therapist can precisely pinpoint the area needing treatment. After treatment they provide a history of the patient's treatment areas to future healthcare providers." (From the website of Texas Oncology/ Dr. John T. Gwozdz, M.D.)

"The body never lies." (Martha Graham)

For most of my life, I have tended to go along without giving my body much conscious thought beyond the necessities of nourishment, excretion, and libido. It's really only when something is wrong—head congestion, leg cramp, shortness of breath due to the occasional panic attack—that I really think of my body. Even then, it's usually to think of my body as something separate from me, something impeding my efforts to focus on what I want or need to be focused on.

As I enter middle age, though, I find that I've been thinking about my body more and more frequently. I never used to have allergies, for example, but now take Claritin at least once a day in the spring. Riding a bicycle—which was, for the longest time, my preferred method of transportation—now results in more fatigue than it used to. Not too very long ago, lying on the couch with my head in my wife's lap while watching a movie, I suffered a back spasm that caused me to bolt upright and cross my arms in front of myself. She grabbed for the phone, thinking I was having a heart attack.

So I've been considering my body, and spending more time looking at it in the mornings, before getting into the shower. I used to avoid doing this—as a young man, it was bad for my self-image to acknowledge the lack of muscle tone and—at various times—either scrawniness of beer-bloated heaviness of my upper body. But if I must be an old man—and apparently, that's going to be my fate—I feel obligated to look at myself and honestly deal with what I see.

As a nonfiction writer, I suppose I'm most struck by the way my body can be read as a narrative of illness and injury. My oldest markings appear on the right-hand side of my body, and tell the story of foolish accidents from childhood. In my right hip there is a small grayish-blue dot that used to be bigger, but hasn't quite faded away. This is graphite from the tip of a pencil, jammed into my side while shooting a free-throw during a school ground basketball game. I had forgotten that the pencil was in my pocket, and when I fell forward after putting all of my strength into the shot, the pencil jabbed its way through the fabric of the shorts I was wearing and into my side. I guess the injury must have been pretty severe—I remember going to the family doctor over it, but not the emergency room. The memory has faded as surely as the wound has healed, but there's still that tiny dot.

There's also the hypertrophic scar just below my right elbow, from the time I took the steepest hill in our neighborhood on my ten-speed, only to discover that my brakes didn't work quite as well as I needed them to in order to attempt such a feat. I went careening, ass over handlebars, into my neighbors' mailbox, knocking it down and messing up my bike's chain in the process. Luckily, the neighbors were on vacation. To this day, I doubt they know why their mailbox mysteriously "fell down." Though I suspected that I needed stitches for the deep cut in my arm, I just went home and put a big Band-Aid on it. I didn't want to get into trouble for taking out the neighbor's mailbox, after all.

The stories told by these scars seem kind of quaint, maybe even silly, in hindsight. At the time, I'm sure I thought I had experienced great pain, but that was nothing compared to the tales the scars on my left could tell you.

The first and most obvious scar would be the one on my neck, which is actually three different scars from three different lymph node biopsies. I was diagnosed with cancer—Hodgkin's Disease—three times between the ages of 21 and 24, and these indentations that line my neck tell at least part of the story of those early adulthood years—hours spent kneeling in front of the toilet, the baseball hat that filled with my own shed hair in one afternoon, the lonely, terror-filled nights that eventually turned into exhausted mornings.

I have a smaller biopsy scar inside my right thigh, near my groin. This biopsy was done several years later, after a routine scan suggested that I had a mass growing there. It turned out to be a mistake, but I have this small line there to remind me of the time that we thought my cancer had not only come back, but had moved south.

I don't tend to notice these markings very often—they're simply a part of that body that, as I mentioned before, I tend not to think about. I'm not sure that most people who see them even notice them—nobody has ever asked me about them, anyway. But people do tend to ask about the dots on my chest, splitting me right down the middle, when they see me without a shirt on. This doesn't happen too often as I get older and spend less time at swimming pools or water parks, but every girlfriend I've had since 2000 has, at some point, rested her head against my bare shoulder and pointed to one, asking, "What are these?" They look like freckles, only blue.

I'd always wanted to have a tattoo, but I've never been able to come up with a design that really expresses something important to me. I know that some people memorialize dead loved ones by inscribing their names on their skin, but I don't really have a dead loved one who I can honestly say meant so much to me that it would justify such a permanent reminder. An ex-girlfriend has the name of her two kids on her leg. That seems cool, but I don't have kids, I have cats. Getting a cat's name tattooed on one's body just seems ridiculous. One friend of mine—a professor of Religion and very devout Christian—has the Greek words for "sin" and "grace" tattooed on his upper arm. That's a cool tattoo—personally important, but also rather scholarly. I'd like a tattoo like that, but all that comes to mind for me and my life are quotes by essayists. "Que sais-je?" "A writer is always selling somebody out." "As a writing man, or secretary, I have always felt charged with the safekeeping of all unexpected items of worldly and unworldly enchantment, as though I might be held personally responsible if even a small one were to be lost." But these feel more pretentious than genuinely expressive of my own personality or interests—although I must admit that the last one, written by E.B. White in "The Ring of Time," is sort of tempting. I have a feeling it would be a good conversation starter if I could unbutton my shirt at the hotel bar at the next academic conference to display that emblazoned across my chest.

So, no artistic, intellectual, or spiritual tattoo for me. But, as I said, there are the blue dots. These were administered by a medical technician with a needle in February of 2000, when I was diagnosed with cancer for the third and—so far, at least—final time. Chemotherapy—both conventional and more aggressive—had failed to destroy my malignancy, so the decision was made that I should be treated with radiation. As we all know, radiation can be very effective at curing cancers, but also effective at causing cancers as well. For this reason, doctors are careful about pointing the radiation beam directly and specifically at the area of the body that contains the malignant mass. To help calibrate their radiation machine, they draw targets on the patient's body—for me, those targets were tiny blue dots that go down my chest. My tattoos.

These little dots are not quite as explicitly spiritual as my friend the religion professor's markings or as emotionally resonant as my ex-girlfriend's kids' names, but I have to say, they matter to me. When I do happen to notice them, or when I do have to explain them, they call to mind all sorts of important things. They remind me of my mortality, which can be depressing but also inspiring—the knowledge that we don't have much time is an admonishment not to waste any.

More than that, though, they remind me of the absolute worst months of my life. I spent eight weeks getting treatments that caused me to vomit and that resulted in the skin on my chest and back burning and cracking, seeping blood and pus. I had no family nearby at that point, and though I had many good friends who tried to help me, they were also living their lives while I—for the only time in my life—was thinking seriously about ending mine. I spent my days eating Wheat Thins and drinking Hawaiian Punch—- nothing else appealed to my tumultuous stomach or enflamed throat. I sat around listening to Warren Zevon's version of Steve Winwood's "Back in the High Life Again," which at the time was the saddest song I knew.

Why on earth, you might ask, would I want to be reminded of such a time? Perhaps for the same reason that my friend the Christian displays his faith on his skin or my ex-girlfriend the single mom has her kids on hers: Gratitude. Appreciation. It has been fifteen years since I finished these treatments. As my health returned, I vowed to never forget, to try to be a better person. But in the decade-plus that's transpired since then, I have largely failed in those endeavors. I still lose my temper in traffic. I still forget to clean the cat's litter box despite promising my wife I would do it. I still have inconsiderate or selfish moments that disappoint, frustrate, and anger others. Don't get me wrong—I'm not a monster, and I never was. But I can do better.

So my tattoos—these blue dots down my chest that mark me as someone who has suffered, held onto his life, and promised himself that he would make that life count for something—remind me to do just that: better. Better than the self-centered person I know I can be. Better than the lazy guy who shuts his office door and screws around on Facebook when he is supposed to be writing. Better than the short-tempered professor who sometimes feels personally insulted when his students fail an assignment. Better than the forgetful husband who unintentionally breaks his promises. Better than I am. The blue dots—like the other markings on my body—ultimately remind me of my own frailty, and the need to live a life that I won't regret, once it's over. These markings tell the story of my life. What's more, they remind me of the story's moral.

Chrononaut

Flash: You see, this treadmill is cosmic-ray powered! And it is coordinated with radiation pulses from the cosmic ray clock! When the treadmill goes forward, positive radiation is released—and that sends me into the future! When it goes backward, negative pulses are released, and that hurls me back to the past! Of course, each of these moments, I am traveling at super-speed—as fast as I can go! But now, Wally—you and I both have to do some time-traveling! Go get into your Kid Flash uniform and while I get into mine I'll tell you about what I've discovered!

Kid Flash: Jumping Jets!

From *The Flash* #125—"The Conquerors of Time," written by John Broome and drawn by Carmine Infantino and Joe Giella. Published in 1961 by DC Comics.

At some point around the fall of 2003—three years after my final treatments for Hodgkin's Disease lymphoma—I began to experience the past again. It would be inaccurate to call these episodes flashbacks. When I hear that term, I always think of veterans who temporarily believe that they are back in a warzone and lash out at innocent bystanders. But it would be similarly inaccurate to dismiss these sensations as mere nostalgia. I would be sitting at my desk, writing or grading student papers, and suddenly I'd feel overwhelmed with the memory of, say, the smell of incense in the dorm my freshman year of college, or a cheesy pop song that they used to play at the roller skating rink when I was in elementary school. And I'd have to set my pen down, take my glasses off, and sigh with the realization that I was remembering something from my life that I'd forgotten and would no doubt forget again.

Cancer researchers have noted a phenomenon called "chemo brain," though there's no real evidence to suggest that the symptoms are caused by chemotherapy—maybe it's a side-effect of radiation therapy, or anti-nausea drugs. It could also be a purely psychological response to the stress of having a serious disease, of thinking about death and life and family and money and the knowledge that it's suddenly very important to think very, very hard about everything. It all matters when you're sick, even the stuff that you never paid much attention to before. Regardless, though, it seems to be a very real, very common experience among cancer patients. Essentially, cognitive ability becomes disrupted, and memories—usually short-term—wind up lost. Patients report that they frequently have difficulty performing tasks that used to be quite easy—reading, concentrating on a crossword puzzle, even choosing the appropriate words to express an idea. Although this may not seem like such a big deal—who really cares if one says "I feel all...spinny" instead of "I'm experiencing dizziness" when one's white blood cell counts are dangerously low?—for the patient it can be both frustrating and frightening.

I had experienced the "chemo brain" phenomenon, and found that, though most of the obvious symptoms went away in the months that followed my bone marrow transplant, years later I still couldn't shake the feeling that I had once been smarter, more focused, better able to think logically and articulate those thoughts coherently. It wasn't too bad—I was able to finish my master's degree and begin a Ph.D. program, so I couldn't have been *so* dumb—but I found myself suddenly susceptible to musings about music or movies or sex or grocery shopping when I was supposed to be listening to a professor give a lecture about Michel Foucault. It wasn't, I realized, that I was uninterested or bored—I just seemed to lack some type of consciousness filter that I used to have, that had allowed me to observe even mundane things with clarity.

But, as I said, this wasn't too much of a problem. At least, not until the fall of 2003, when just as I was taking steps towards a more certain future for myself with a career path and a girlfriend I planned to marry, I was suddenly overwhelmed by events and sensations from the past. Friends, teachers, and relatives; vacations, songs, and comic books—they all returned, quite uninvited, and frequently left me feeling overwhelmed and inexplicably sad. The past is forever lost to us—we all know that we don't get to go back and relive our most cherished memories. But being hopelessly pushed towards the future and away from my past seemed sadder and sadder the longer I lived. I was 27.

My favorite superhero when I was a kid was the Flash, and my favorite individual comic book was *Secret Origins* Annual #2, a 64-page mini-epic published in 1988 that recounted the careers of two of the three Flashes—the "Silver Age" Flash of the 1960s and 1970s (police scientist Barry Allen) and the "modern" Flash of the 1980s (Barry's nephew, Wally West, the former Kid Flash who assumed his mentor's superhero identity when Barry was killed traveling through time to defend the earth from the villainous Anti-Monitor). Although I tried hard to keep all of my comics in mint condition—carefully sealed in mylar bags and stored in specially-designed cardboard comic book boxes— that *Secret Origins* annual was so thoroughly read that the cover became crinkled and loose, separated from its staples. I probably read that comic book at least a couple of times a week, and I even brought it with me on long car trips in order to entertain myself with Barry's heroism and Wally's anxiety about living up to his uncle's legend.

It's not hard to see why I loved that character, and that book in particular. While other kids of the 80s were entertained and inspired by Wolverine's violent cynicism or Superman's humble use of his God-like powers in service to mankind, I liked the idea of the guy who could just run really, really fast. In hindsight, I realize that I had always imagined myself as a clean-cut, good-looking, Fellowship of Christian Athletes kind of kid, but I found myself stuck with the body and inclinations of an overweight, morally impure, *Fellowship of the Rings* type of kid, and everybody—friends and family alike—seemed to know it even better than I did. Though I would have loved to hold hands with the pretty girls in school or give my dad some evidence of athletic prowess to brag about to the other men at his country club, that just didn't seem to be me.

But, my favorite comic book reminded me, everybody thought that Barry Allen was a nerd and a slow-poke too. He hung around in a lab all day. His girlfriend rode her bike faster than he rode his, leaving him in her dust. He wore a bow tie, for heaven's sake. He was probably a bigger geek than I was—except for when he wore the red costume with the lightning insignia on its chest. Then, he was the fastest man alive. Decent. Athletic. An American hero.

Although to everyone else I may have appeared to be a complete dork, the Flash reminded me that I didn't have to be limited to that reality. My secret identity was someone awesome, and if—like Barry—I had to keep that knowledge to myself, well, nobody said that being a hero would be easy.

Slightly less appealing but still important, I'm sure, is that Barry was able to run fast enough—with the aid of his physics-defying "cosmic treadmill"—to travel through time. Back then, I liked the idea of journeying to the future, to the day when I would leave behind my fat and my zits and my clumsiness, to the day when the world would already love me as my truer, more attractive and noble self. I wasn't too interested in going to the past to see dinosaurs or Abraham Lincoln, but I was fairly obsessed with getting over being a kid, and getting to the point where I would be the muscular, handsome young hero with the perfect teeth and beautiful girlfriend. And if the year 1999 had flying cars too, hey, so much the better.

The semester ended peacefully, with my grading done well ahead of the university's deadline for final grade submissions. I was spending less and less time at my own apartment, preferring to hang out at Emily's place. My "melancholic memory episodes" were still occurring, but never when I was with her.

One afternoon while Emily was busy with her own grading, I was in my apartment trying to get some writing done when my mother called. This was odd, because she did not frequently call me—usually, I would call her on a Wednesday or Thursday afternoon (or early in the morning in Hawaii, where they lived). She would share the latest news and gossip from the family, update me on how my siblings were doing, and we would usually hang up after a half hour or so. But, as I said, I called her—she never called me. So when I saw my parents' phone number on the caller ID, I knew that it probably wasn't good news.

"Your grandmother's in the hospital," she told me when I answered the phone.

"Is it serious?" I asked, mostly for something to say. My mom's not one for drama. She wouldn't have called if it weren't serious.

"Your father flew out this morning," she answered.

So this was it. My father hadn't flown out for his mother's previous hospitalization, so it must have been made clear to him that the time to see her was now.

"Is he okay?" I asked.

She hesitated before answering noncommittally, "This isn't really a surprise."

"Are you going to join him?"

"I can't," she answered. "Your sister's going to be here tonight."

My sister had been struggling with depression and anxiety problems for quite some time, and she and my parents had agreed weeks before that she would finish up the semester at New Mexico State University and then come back to stay with them for a while. Though I had known about this plan, it also seemed to me that, with my grandmother's recent turn for the worse, the plan might have been altered.

"We really want her to just get out here so we can take care of her," my mom said.

"So you didn't tell her before she got on the plane?"

"She's been so upset," my mom said, in a tone that told me she wasn't sure if she'd made the right decision or not. My sister had lived with my grandmother for a while, back when her depression compelled her to seek out family that lived in the continental United States, and the two of them had become close.

"That makes sense," I assured her quickly. "She's better off with you."

"That's what we thought."

"Yeah." I couldn't escape the feeling that my mom was waiting for me to say something, like we were working from a script and I should have been off-book. "So... Dad's flying out by himself."

"Yeah."

Would a more sensitive person know what his line was supposed to be? Was my brain so fried by chemotherapy or radiation or illness-related stress that I'd forgotten something as important as what a man says to his mother in this situation? Or was this the type of conversation that's impossible to prepare for?

"Should I go to New Mexico to be with him?" I asked.

I expected this to be an empty gesture, for her to say, "Oh, no—that's not necessary." Instead, she asked, "Could you?"

So in this way the matter was decided. I would go over to Emily's that night—we were hosting an end-of-semester/Christmas party—and then the next morning I would get in the car and start driving towards Carlsbad, New Mexico to be with my father at my dying grandmother's bedside.

"I wish you didn't have to go," Emily said as I told her of the new plan. It wasn't selfishness—she wasn't trying to say that I should ignore my father, or shun my grandmother on her deathbed. It was said simply as a statement of her desire. She wished that we could have these days after grades were handed in together, to watch movies and get drunk and spend all day in bed, as we'd planned. That's the promise of the end of the semester, after all—you've got a week or so of constant work, but you know that it's eventually going to end, and that you'll have several days without responsibilities to just relax. But we both knew that as much as you try to make plans, the future isn't always what you want it to be.

I was nine years old when I built my first time machine. It was 1985. My best friend, Byron, and I had just seen *Back to the Future*, I was spending the night at his house, and we both had well-developed imaginations. Since he already had a go-kart which was, admittedly, not quite as cool as a DeLorean, it made sense to convert it into a vehicle for time travel.

Scientists say that time travel is purely theoretical, that building a time machine is really, really difficult, but don't you believe it. Byron and I found that all it took was cannibalizing my old Speak-N-Spell for colorful wires and duct-taping a calculator to the go-kart's hood. Honestly, the whole process couldn't have taken more than ten minutes. Since it was Byron's go-kart, he got to sit in the driver's seat and punch the coordinates into what used to be the calculator. But since we weren't actually moving through physical space, it didn't matter that I wasn't behind the steering wheel anyway. We sat and waited for a moment before looking around the garage we were sitting in.

"Did we do it?" I asked.

"I think so," Byron answered, looking around. "Oh, yeah. Definitely. The garage wasn't this messy when we left."

"Oh yeah," I said, noticing that fact for the first time.

We walked out of the garage and into the summer night. At least I assumed it was summer—it had been summer when we left, and I was still comfortable in my short sleeves.

"Let's split up and explore," Byron said, walking towards the gate that led to the alley behind the house that had been his back in 1985.

I guess I was nervous about venturing too far from the time machine—what if Byron got back and couldn't find me? I'd be trapped in…wait. He hadn't told me if we'd gone to the past or the future. So I looked around, trying to figure out just when I was.

The elm tree looked about as big as it had in 1985, so, I reasoned, we probably weren't in the past. Plus, whoever lived in Byron's house still had a pool, and I was pretty sure Byron's parents had installed that when they moved in. So this had to be the future.

I walked closer to the house and peered through the living room window. Whoever lived there now hadn't changed much about the living room décor. Same lamps, same carpet. Even the piano was in the same place. And that's when I got my biggest shock—Byron's mother came into the room and started playing the piano—just like she would have done in 1985.

It was difficult to come up with an explanation to allow myself to hold onto the idea that I'd travelled through time, but I figured it out. Obviously, Byron's older sister—who also played the piano—had kept their parents' house. And there she was, the spitting image of her mom, seated at the same piano her mother had played all those years ago. Byron would no doubt be pleased by my reasoning.

It took him a little while to get back, but when he did I enthusiastically shared all I had discovered.

"That's odd," he said. "You went into the future, but I went into the past."

"What do you mean?" I asked.

"I found a garbage can that had all sorts of old magazines in it. So I know I was in the past."

"But how? If I went to the future?"

Byron thought for a moment, then said, "We must have ripped a hole in the space-time continuum when we activated the time machine."

"Oh no!"

"We'd better get back to 1985 right away."

I'm pleased to tell you that we made it back safe and sound, and that the space-time continuum seems none the worse for wear. And I suppose it made sense that Byron went to the past and I went to the future—he was probably smarter than me, and more curious about history, whereas I liked to daydream about a world of robots and jetpacks.

It seems a shame, though, that I hadn't actually seen anything useful about the future on our one and only trip through time. If I had, I might've been able to brace myself for the fact that, the following summer, my parents would announce that we were moving away, and that I'd never see Byron again. I might have warned him, too, that his mom would die that same summer. I might have learned something about what was to come that might have made us appreciate the world we had at the time.

But I suppose every grown-up says that about childhood, even if he didn't build a time machine with his best friend when he was a kid. And perhaps it's better just to focus on the fun we had later in the summer, when we both saw *Teen Wolf* and took to growling at each other at every full moon.

We all experience death at some time or another. There's our own, of course, but few of us escape from this world without having to keep a vigil accompanied by the steady beeping of a heart monitor, or asking a doctor "What are her chances?" or attending a funeral. So I probably don't need to tell you about hugging my father as he cried, or my grandfather's inability to speak when he visited his wife in her hospital room, or about kissing her forehead after she was gone. These are things we do.

But I do need to tell you about my own thoughts the night before she died. My uncle, my aunt, and my father had taken turns sitting by her side, holding her hand, making sure she was never left alone. They were, of course, exhausted, so my cousin and I agreed that we would take the 9 p.m. to 2 a.m. vigil. I tend to stay up late anyway, so the hours didn't bother me, and as long as my cousin was there, I felt confident that the experience wouldn't be overwhelmingly depressing. I feared being alone with my grandmother, I'll admit—I didn't want to be the only person in the room when she died. In fact, I would have preferred not to be in the room at all when she died—I wasn't sure how I would react to seeing someone just disappear, no longer exist. But as long as I wasn't alone, I figured I could handle it.

Naturally, though, my cousin didn't show up until 11:00. He'd gone to a movie with his girlfriend, and hadn't realized that *The Lord of the Rings: The Two Towers* would be so long. By the time he strolled in, sucking down a 64-ounce soda through a straw, I'd been sitting there—holding her hand, occasionally lifting a cup of water to her lips, watching her die slowly—for two hours.

It was not an altogether horrifying experience, as I'd feared. Periodically, she would stop breathing, then start back up again, which meant that alarms frequently went off to attract the attention of ICU nurses who seemed to know to ignore the noise unless it went on for a set amount of time. Since I didn't know how much time was too much, I jumped in my seat every time the alarm sounded, then watched the door anxiously to see if someone came in before it stopped.

She occasionally woke up, too, which was nice and eerie at the same time. She congratulated me on getting engaged. (Did she realize that she wouldn't be attending the wedding?) She looked at the engagement photos I'd brought with me. (Did she remember that the last time I visited her—three years before—I was dating a different good-looking blond woman?) Once, she opened her eyes and looked at me quizzically. "Joe?" she asked. Joe is my father's name. And her deceased first husband's. "What?" I asked, not sure what the appropriate thing to say was. "Oh," she said, closing her eyes again. "You're Billy." Nobody had called me that in about fifteen years, but it didn't seem all that odd to me. Clichéd narrative would have us believe that our lives flash before our eyes when we die, so if she was somewhere in the past while talking to me, I suppose it would be understandable. I had, after all, been taking frequent mental trips to the past myself in recent months.

When I was sick and stuck in a hospital bed, I self-consciously did not entertain the notion that my situation was somehow unfair. In fact, death—which Hamlet pointed out happens to beggars as well as kings—is the great equalizer; it's evidence of the universe's fundamental Marxism. In our mortality, we are all made equal. So though illness and death angered and terrified me, I tried to keep from feeling victimized by my own humanity.

But, really, I'm also of the generation that grew up with videotapes and audio cassettes; the rewind button's promise of endless repetition had deceived me to the point that what *did* seem unfair was that I couldn't experience this movie again.

And so, though I felt comfortable enough with the knowledge that my grandmother would die, that my father would die, that Emily would die, and that I would die, the fact that I couldn't go back and visit the guy I once was—that I couldn't have that first flirtatious conversation with Emily, or feel my dad's arms around me as he showed me how to hold a golf club, or spend endless summers in the home of a grandmother who loved and spoiled me—disappointed me beyond words.

If I'd had a cosmic treadmill like the Flash's, I thought to myself while my grandmother slept, I wouldn't make selfish use of it. Not really. I wouldn't use it to make money or manufacture prestige. I wouldn't even travel to the future to try to find technology that could revitalize her weakening heart. She had raised her kids, saw the births of several great-grandkids, buried one husband, and lived into her eighties despite a lifetime of smoking and red meat. She'd had a good run, and—to her credit—she didn't seem particularly scared about what was to come next. She had to die, because she had lived. This was right and fair.

But if I'd had that cosmic treadmill, I would have hopped on and started running. Not forward, towards the future, as I would have when I was a kid; my life was already a time machine taking me towards the future. No, I would have run backwards, through the early parts of the current century—when I didn't really see her much at all. Back through the nineties, where I could see myself walking in reverse, away from the doctor's office where I was diagnosed with my cancer, away from that first serious girlfriend who broke my heart, loved me, and had sex with me for the first time—in that order, from this point-of-view—away from the terrifying adult world after receiving my diploma at high school graduation. I'd go all the way back to the summer of 1988—a summer spent in her air conditioned house in New Mexico, swimming with my cousins, playing hide-and-seek, drinking iced tea and reading my favorite superhero's secret origin over and over again, delighting in it each time. And the only thing I would change, maybe, was that when my grandmother came into the room holding her cigarette and smiling at me, I wouldn't act put out when she asked me to put the comic book down and come outside with her. Instead, I'd say "Okay," content in the knowledge that the Flash would still be there later, in the future. It's dangerous to change the past on a time travel mission, but such a small change, such a tiny historical correction, would not likely pose too much of a threat to the space-time continuum.

But I have no cosmic treadmill, nor a DeLorean equipped with a flux capacitor, nor even a go-kart modified with a calculator and a Speak and Spell. So she died the day after my vigil at her bedside, and my other grandmother died the following year, and—as someone rooted in the present and moving towards the future—I'll never be a person who has a grandmother again.

My apartment was clean when I got home from New Mexico. Spotless, in fact. Which was funny, because I had left a stack of dishes in the kitchen sink, beard trimmings in the bathroom sink, and overflowing garbage cans in most of the rooms. Even the floors had been cleaned.

My first response was not gratitude. I hated to think of Emily cleaning up after me, feared that she would come to resent me if she had to pick up my messes. As a man committed to feminist principles, I didn't expect her to give up her career, or her autonomy, or her last name when she married me. And I certainly didn't feel like she should have to spray and scrub the mildew out from my tub's grout. I felt like a jerk for leaving so much clutter in my wake for her to tidy up. And I was enough of a jerk to feel like she was a little bit responsible for making me feel like a jerk.

"You really shouldn't have," I told her when she answered the phone.

"It was no trouble," she replied.

"Yeah, but…I just wish you wouldn't clean up my messes. That's not your responsibility."

"I know," she answered. "But I missed you, and I wanted to do something nice for you, and it was all I could think of."

"Well…thank you."

"I'm never washing your dishes again, though. That was kinda gross."

"Yeah. Sorry about that."

"Are you coming over?"

Of course I was.

At some point, those flashes from the past stopped. I'm not sure when it happened—I'm pretty sure it wasn't until some point after the wedding—but I feel like it's for the best. As much as I value my memories, and as important as I believe personal history is, nostalgia can be dangerous. A longing for the past frequently translates into a loathing for the present, and a fear of the future. And I don't want to become one of those miserable old bastards, saying things like, "You call that music? In *my* day, we had C & C Music Factory and Salt-N-Peppa. Now *that* was music."

Don't get me wrong—I still love the comic books of yesteryear, and have quite a collection of comics from the early 70s up through the mid-90s. There's a certain joy that comes with reacquainting myself with the person I was—the kid who couldn't imagine a braver sacrifice than the one Barry Allen made to save his loved ones, and who liked to fancy that he could be capable of heroism, too, put in the same fantastic situation. But while the past is a fun and interesting place to visit, I have no desire to live there. I'm content to move forward—slowly, not on the treadmill—into an uncertain future with someone who likes to do nice things for me, but knows to draw the line at gross dishes left in the sink. The present isn't perfect and the future can be unpredictable, but I'm content with my life, and still in love with the person I'm sharing it with. And in some very significant ways, that's better that having a robot butler or a flying car.

Flash: C-Can't bear...to look! So many...memories! So... terribly vivid!! I wish...I wish that I could do it all over again!! I wish that my life was just beginning! But all that I can hope for now is a happy ending!

From *Secret Origins* Annual #2— "Mystery of the Human Thunderbolt," written by Robert Loren Fleming and drawn by Carmine Infantino and Murphy Anderson. Published in 1988 by DC Comics.

First Thing

My Hodgkin's Disease had returned—my doctor was fairly certain. This was in 2006, six years after my last radiation treatment. This time it was in my thigh rather than in my neck and chest area, but nonetheless, it was back. I would need to have a biopsy performed, of course, but that was just a formality. A hunk of lymph nodes would be cut out, and then we'd begin treatments—likely radiation therapy, but a bone marrow transplant remained a possibility as well. Time was of the essence. I was likely going to die. Emily and I had serious thinking to do.

It turned out to be a false alarm—my cancer hadn't come back at all. I lived, and I obviously continue to live. The strange glows on the scan were… well, something other than cancer. But we didn't know that at the time.

What we did know was that, when I'd had my bone marrow transplant in 1998, my doctor had said that I had a 40% chance of living for more than five years. We also knew that I had radiation therapy to treat a recurrence two years after the transplant. Emily and I didn't meet until after I had completed these treatments, but we had discussed my medical history, and what it meant for our relationship, once we began "seriously" dating. When we met in grad school we tried to keep things relatively casual at first so that we wouldn't be tied down to another person. Neither of us wanted to compromise on our professional ambitions by becoming too attached to someone similarly ambitious, so we self-consciously tried to limit our relationship to one of hanging out and hooking up—a bit more intimate than "friends with benefits," but nothing too emotionally consequential. But at some point while hiking through the Missouri wilderness, or discussing the latest academic scandal reported in *The Chronicle of Higher Education* over coffee, or drinking cheap wine in her small basement apartment, we fell in love with each other, and decided the best thing to do would be to get married. I couldn't quite tell you when I realized that she mattered more to me than keeping all of my options open for the sake of my career, but I know that it happened.

Our life together was filled with reading, writing, sending out academic articles and creative work, supporting each other when the eventual rejections came, applying for academic jobs, worrying about money. We also played Scrabble, sought out strange landmarks like the world's largest statue of a goose ("Maxie" in Sumner, Missouri), watched livestock shows at state fairs, and—in the words of the girl in Hemingway's "Hills Like White Elephants"—we would "look at things and try new drinks."

We had both been in relationships before we met each other, of course. Both of us had been in college relationships that had continued for far too long, with protracted break-ups and broken hearts. After my bone marrow transplant, as my college girlfriend and I were breaking up for the final time, I reflected on what I wanted in a romantic relationship. Someone adventurous, willing to travel and have new experiences. Someone who loved literature as much as I did, but who could also enjoy the same type of lowbrow culture I enjoyed—I wanted to be able to talk about books and art with someone who could appreciate the sublime genius of Don Knotts's performance in *The Ghost and Mr. Chicken*. Someone who had a sense of humor, who would laugh if I called her "scumbag" and would be willing to high-five me after sex. In short, I wanted to be in a relationship that was fun—I'd had enough of passive-aggression and adolescent angst.

As it happens, Emily had recently reached similar conclusions about her own love life. It wasn't love at first sight, but we immediately knew that we made each other laugh and had fun together—she was not only down with the high-fiving, but was willing to call me "dude." Things grew from there.

As Emily and I contemplated what a malignancy would mean for our relationship, I realized I couldn't really say that life was unfair. I had been fortunate to be disease-free for as long as I had been, I figured, and I had experienced a powerful love and friendship the likes of which I don't think too many people get to experience. The only disappointment was that we couldn't make it last forever. It looked like our time together was coming to an end.

In the week between the tentative diagnosis and the biopsy that would ultimately be reassuring, we spent our days crying, our evenings drinking wine and trying to reassure each other that this would be okay, nothing we couldn't handle. I'd done all this before, with only my parents for companionship and support. With her—and with them providing support from a distance— it wouldn't be nearly as bad. She would take care of me. I would not have to feel isolated, the way I had when I was treated before. Together, we would manage. We said these things to each other, but hanging between us—unspoken, but mutually understood— was the understanding that a recurrence at this point could very well mean I would die.

The morning of the biopsy, Emily drove me to the hospital. After the nurse called me from the waiting room to the pre-op area, I handed Emily my wedding ring, which she put on her thumb. I kissed her goodbye.

What followed seemed to take forever—the shaving, the pre-surgery talk with the doctor, then watching the anesthesia drip through my IV.

I shut my eyes, then opened them to find myself sitting up, in recovery. It happened that fast. Emily and a nurse were laughing. I had a Diet Coke and a glass of water in front of me— my usual beverage order, if I'm not drinking wine or beer.

"Where did this Diet Coke and water come from?" I asked.

Emily smiled. "You asked the nurse for them when you woke up after your surgery."

"Oh," I replied. "I must have thought I was at a restaurant."

At this, both Emily and the nurse exploded in laughter again.

"That's the fourth time you've asked that question," Emily said, "and then followed with 'I must have thought I was at a restaurant.'"

I laughed too—although I should tell you that, later, when we told the story to friends, they were horrified. "I would have been afraid that it was permanent," one friend replied. That obviously hadn't occurred to Emily—or else, she is so used to the way I am normally, she didn't worry that any lasting brain damage would be noticeable or change her life in any fundamental way.

At one point—still foggy and a bit confused—I glanced down at my left hand. My wedding ring was back where it belonged.

"When did you give this back to me?" I asked, holding up my hand.

This time, Emily did not laugh as she ran her hand up and down on my arm, telling me that it was the first thing I'd asked for—before the beverages, even—when I saw her after coming out of surgery.

"You said that you missed it," she told me.

Emily and I have been together for 12 years, and as happy as that time has been, I have to tell you that we argue as much as any couple. Maybe even more—we can both be strong-willed and opinionated, especially when it comes to matters of teaching and writing, which are important parts of our careers. Sometimes, we argue over a work of literature. Sometimes, it's pop culture. We rarely argue about politics, but it happens, sometimes.

More rarely—but more seriously—we fight about the important things in our marriage. Whether one of us takes the other for granted. Occasions of self-centeredness. Concerns that one of us prioritizes work over our relationship with each other. These are the serious fights. The ones that result in tears for her, or me stomping out of the house to "Go for a walk, to clear my head." These are the times when we get overwhelmed with thought—fears, suspicions, and pressures that probably come from outside the marriage itself, but are nonetheless real, as we contemplate them.

But what I like about the story of my recovery from surgery is that it testifies to the fact that loving her isn't something I have to think about—that even when my mind is wrapped up in a confused fog, when I'm basically just a being incapable of reflection, operating on instinct and biological imperative, I still love her. More than I love my job, more than I love literature, more than I love anything in the world. And I love her first, even before I get my Diet Coke and glass of water.

Peace Through More Power Than A Locomotive

"What is the ape to men? A laughingstock or painful embarrassment. And just so shall man be to Superman: a laughingstock or painful embarrassment." (Friedrich Nietzche)

I t's easy to be impressed by Superman, but sometimes I think he holds back too much. No question, Metropolis is a safer city for having him in it, and the world's probably a better place, having him to guard it against invasions from Apokolips or Brainiac's death rays. But really, how many times does Earth encounter a truly existential threat? How much good does the guy really do, confronting bank robbers who, when their bullets bounce off his chest, literally throw their guns at him? He could be doing so much more.

If I had Superman's powers, man, I'd change the world for the better. I'd use my powers to literally clean up the town—not just rid the streets of crime, but also take care of pollution. Overflowing landfills matter little to someone who can just throw abandoned refrigerators and old tires into the heart of the sun, after all. And what's more, I could lead by example, talking to people about the importance of conservation. I could use my superpowers and my super-rhetorical skills to persuade my neighbors that they should follow my lead, and consider allowing me to represent them in some type of elected office. Start out small—say, a town council election. Or perhaps the school board.

I'd make a point of listening to all sides before taking any sort of stand, and the public would know that their champion and defender is a man who is fair to all, yet who is steadfast in his convictions. Even those who disagreed with me would have to allow that I'm principled. And I'd do a good job, making my community an even nicer place in which to live and raise a family, because, gosh darn it, I'm a hard-working progressive superhero whose intentions are pure and noble.

Once successful at the local level, I would amass enough goodwill to bring my crusade to the larger world. Other communities have landfills of their own, of course. And criminals who need to be brought to justice. What's more, think of all the nuclear waste out there, poisoning the land. Who's going to take care of that? Why, your Man of Steel is going to take care of that. It might not be safe to launch a bunch of nuclear waste into the heart of the sun—honestly, I'd like to talk to some of the world's best scientific minds, like Neil DeGrasse Tyson and Dr. Ray "The Atom" Palmer to find out for sure—but Great Krypton, I could just send the stuff into the Phantom Zone, where it would never be able to bother us. And then we could continue to work on other, cleaner substitutes—perhaps using my own body as an example of an efficient, powerful solar battery.

Of course, it's not enough to just solve these problems using muscles and my own technology. I'd need to lead the way in terms of shifting the public consciousness, encouraging people to think in the correct ways. I'd make sure to get myself in front of the television cameras to promote my vision for a better, kinder, more just world. I'd have a sense of humor about myself too. Too many liberals can be so positively shrill and unlikeable, even when—hell, especially when— they're trying to be funny. Maybe, as a gag, I could appear on TV and let people throw guns at me—maybe even the guns that I'd helped criminalize and confiscate.

I'd inspire people with good deeds, pithy slogans, and a detailed, thoroughly studied understanding of any given issue. I'd earn their trust and love, and the people would, eventually, put me in charge completely.

From there, I would make the case for serious financial sector reform. Never again would a bank be "Too Big to Fail," and I would work to bring our country back to the Keynesian economic policies that made us as strong as we were for the second half of the twentieth century. No more legislation written by out-of-touch billionaires. No more offshore bank accounts for corporate raiders who want to do business in America. And needless to say, single-payer health care for all. Some may have their doubts, but I am certain that such a system would benefit our economy in the long run.

Naturally, some people will compare my ambitions with those of Barack Obama's, when he was a charismatic senator from Illinois. And no doubt some people will say that they were disappointed with President Obama's accomplishments while in office. Some good stuff happened, some not-so-good stuff happened, but in the end they didn't get the utopia they thought they were voting for when they elected him. So why should they put their faith in me?

Well, the truth is, President Obama had to work with a Congress filled with people who didn't trust him. On the other hand, I'm Superman—the only people who don't trust me are megalomaniacal villains like Lex Luthor and Rupert Murdoch. So no worries there. Whereas Obama had to deal with people demanding to personally see his birth certificate at every campaign stop, most earthlings know that I don't even have a birth certificate, and they don't really care. I gave my life to stop Doomsday, for the love of Brando!

(I mean, I got better, but still).

I'd pursue my vision of what this country should be—what is best for the people, whether they realize it or not—with a fundamentalist's zeal, knocking out my opponents as surely as Muhammad Ali knocked me out when the aliens from Scrubb forced us to fight each other (the fight took part on the Scrubb home planet, which has a red sun, so... not my best day). I am convinced that—like the Scrubb boxing enthusiasts who were inspired by the nobility of Ali and my own heroism to depose their maniacal leader—those who might have distrusted me at first would come around when they saw how much better my way is. Once they saw the power of my conviction, the virtue of my positions, the heat of my vision.

Seriously, can you imagine someone looking me in the eye and demanding to see my birth certificate, or suggesting that I hate "earth culture," or that I'm a fascist, knowing that I have heat vision that could melt their eyes in their sockets?

People might disagree at first, but they would come around, and the ends would justify the means. And those unreasonable few who would *still* refuse and resist my utopia? Well... we'd think of something, I'm sure. Perhaps send them to the Phantom Zone with the rest of the waste. I mean, we can't have them polluting our perfect world with their negativity and refusal to consider the big picture.

Okay. Maybe it's for the best that I don't have Superman's powers. I believe in all of my moral and political convictions—I just know, deep down, that I've thought deeply about these issues, that I'm a compassionate man, and that my opinions are just. But I also know, deep down, that the people who disagree with me feel the same way about their own opinions. What's more, I also believe that "I'll make things better and be a hero" is surely the creed that has motivated most of history's monsters, all of whom no doubt started out idealistically, with only the best of intentions.

What the Survey Doesn't Say

"If I never do another thing, I've met the good, sweet people of the world. So I leave you, with love…" (Richard Dawson)

E mily insists that my obsession with the old woman is odd and unreasonable. To be honest, I'm not even sure why she caught my attention, although I guess the fact that I'd been drinking probably played a role. We had finished one bottle of wine and had opened a second when we decided to watch an episode from the *All-Star Family Feud* DVD she'd bought me for my birthday. So maybe that was it—I was too impaired to really pay attention to what was happening with the casts of *The Brady Bunch* and *Petticoat Junction*, and instead found my attention wandering behind Richard Dawson during the final round, over the right shoulder of his black tuxedo, towards the audience and the old lady wearing the red pantsuit.

The first thing I was struck by was that she seemed so very happy to be there. Smiling, clapping, and dressed to the nines (as I imagined they said when she was younger). "How nice for her," I actually said aloud, pointing to the television so that Emily would notice her too—although you really couldn't see much of her and she wasn't on the screen for very long.

But then—and I don't really know why, except maybe I was reminded by seeing Robert Reed on the screen, alive, smiling, quite likely already infected with the horrible virus that would eventually take his life—I remembered how long ago this all happened: 1983. This woman who couldn't have been younger than seventy-five then was seated between two much younger women—daughters? granddaughters? Her husband was, likely, dead and in the ground. As she no doubt was by the time I saw the episode decades later.

I thought it was just the booze making me maudlin that night, but it apparently wasn't, as I find myself thinking of that old woman from time to time even now. She's gone and lost forever, I assume, yet she's still there, on the screen, laughing at Richard Dawson's smarmy attempts at humor, gazing at that ridiculously-large bow tie that must have been fashionable then. And it seems kind of sad to me to think that this woman's immortality depends upon a cynical generation's desire for retro-kitsch. She may have survived the Great Depression. Or the Holocaust. She knew love, I'm sure, and she also knew suffering—maybe cancer, or Alzheimer's disease, or a stroke that made laughter painful and applause impossible. I wonder if she died at home, surrounded by family? Or maybe in a nursing home, alone and scared? Those two younger women were with her at the show, but did they take care of her, or was this just an obligation—"Take the old lady to see her favorite show being taped, and then we're off the hook until Christmas?" Did she know when she got up that morning that this would be a special "All-Star" version of the show, or was it a pleasant surprise, to be able to see Frank Cady and Maureen McCormack at the same time, on the same stage, as Dawson himself? And when all was said and done, was it really that great? Did they deserve the applause? "At the end of your life," I want to ask her, "looking back, did these tiny pleasures make up for the suffering?"

But I guess it's ultimately self-centered for me to make such use of this old lady, conflating her life and death with my own anxieties about time's inevitable forward march and thanatophobia. Part of the reason looking at her makes me sad is that I assume that her own mortality caused misery to outweigh joy in her life. But I don't know that; I didn't ask her. And it's irresponsible to presume that my pessimistic intuition reflects the realities of other people who have lived and died. Anyone who ever lost on the *Family Feud* can tell you that one's own assumptions are not necessarily reflected in the larger survey.

Dislocated

As a writer and reader of essays and memoirs, you know that nearly forty years ago, in his own memoir, Nabokov traced the development of his consciousness to one of his earliest memories, the recognition that he and his parents were distinct human beings. And you know that in *Speak, Memory*, Nabokov often writes of memory as if the recalled events happened to someone else ("… I see my diminutive self…") or as if they are occurring on a movie screen, viewed from his "present ridge of remote, isolated, almost uninhabited time." And though, let's face it, you're never going to be half the writer Nabokov was, you can appreciate this distinction between past and present, between the boy one was and the man one is.

You're loathe to describe your own childhood in the same idyllic terms that Nabokov used to describe his—which is only fair, as he was born to an aristocratic family in the Czar's Russia and you were born to a middle class family in America's Midwest the year before Nabokov himself died. Yet, like Nabokov, you do understand the way that memory has a way of turning the past—forever, tragically lost to all chronophobiacs—into something bright and hopeful, a place where optimism and faith remained unchallenged. If you try hard, you can even remember a time when the world—for you—was a simple place, where moral decisions lacked ambiguity. A world where you always knew—and strived to do—what was right and good and just, in fulfillment of a plan drafted by God and carried out by His servants on earth.

Of course, you're glad for the intellect that allows you to recognize the complexities of the world; you wouldn't really be a grown up if you still viewed the world as if the morality of superhero comic books or Davey and Goliath still seemed relevant. But you can sometimes miss the certainty that living in such a world used to provide, and you can remember it all—the confidence, the faith, the knowledge that God had a clear plan for you and for all— if you try. At the very least, faith once assured you that you weren't alone in the universe.

Shortly after your wedding, you and your wife are nominated to represent her church—your church now, really—at the Synod Assembly. Representatives from Lutheran churches all over the Midwest will be there, and the pastors at St. Andrews think that the two of you would be good representatives of the congregation—if you agree to formally join, which you have been telling your wife you're interested in doing anyway. You were raised Catholic, but the pedophilia scandals and the new Pope's scary, destructive conservatism have convinced you that you can no longer accept spiritual advice from the Vatican.

As happy as you are to be part of a larger spiritual community, though, you're not sure that this Lutheran church is a perfect fit. This discomfort is only heightened when a member of the congregation—an old man who was there when they built the church in the sixties—calls one afternoon in order to "find out how you feel about the issues." Representative to the Synod Assembly is an elected position, after all, voted on by every member of the church. They're only sending four people, and they've got six people running.

"How do you feel about the gay issue?" he wants to know.

"What gay issue?" you ask, dreading the conversation that's about to follow, wherein he will tell you that the gays are filthy, disease-prone, and target children in order to satisfy their twisted desires. And though you're as sensitive and respectful as you can be as you disagree with him, you know that when you tell him, "Actually, we're strongly in favor of legalizing gay marriage" that you've said all he needs to hear; he has already decided that you don't belong, that you're not a child of his God.

Two weeks before that, you are sitting in your doctor's examining room, hoping to be pronounced healthy. You had cancer before, when you were in college, and it has now been five years since your last relapse—assuming the tests come back clear.

When your doctor comes into the room, he is irritatingly guarded (or, perhaps just nonchalant), keeping whatever he knows (if there is anything to know) close to the vest. Most of you is sure that if something had shown up, he would tell you right away, but part of you fears that he's trying to keep you calm, making small talk, waiting to deliver the horrible news. And as he palpitates your neck and listens to your heart, all you can think is, "Please, God. I'll never even look at another cigarette. Or another drink. Or a woman who is not my wife. Just please, please, please." And then the doctor removes the stethoscope from his ears, smiles at you, and extends his hand, congratulating you on your cancer-free status. And you think, "Oh, hell yeah. We're getting wasted tonight."

From five years ago, just after the incident: You're sitting in the psychiatrist's office. He's talking to you about what happened, after the hospital, when you came to your senses in the field, wandering, helpless and thoughtless. The nervous breakdown that followed your appointment with the cancer specialists.

You're wearing your black suit, red shirt with matching tie, and your glasses. You look mature, professional, completely together. And this is by design. You do not want to look like a crazy person, though your hands have been shaking all week and you are fairly convinced that you might be losing your mind.

It started in the examining room, when the social worker assigned to your case a year before entered and began speaking; you hadn't expected to see her there, but she didn't waste any time.

"We're going to admit you tonight," she said. "We'll call your parents, and your sister." Your sister is the only member of your family who is an exact match for a bone marrow transplant, you know from all of the tests conducted in preparation for the worst-case scenario.

"What?" you managed to get out. "Am I sick again?" This was supposed to be a routine follow-up appointment; you'd been in remission for nine months.

She paused for a second, then tilted her head, "Isn't that why you're here?"

It would turn out, later, that there had been a misunderstanding—while you and one of the doctors knew that this was just a check-up, the others had been led to believe that you were returning because of a suspicious spot on a CT scan (a spot which, both you and one doctor knew, was scar tissue from previous surgeries). It was all a terrible misunderstanding, you would learn less than a week later.

That night, however, you started drinking at dinner—two Coronas. Then, your friend Michelle bought you several small bottles of liquor to drink in the car, while she drove and tried to talk to you. You had only finished the first little bottle of Absolut—in fact, you can still remember that the song playing on her CD player was Shania Twain, "Don't Be Stupid." And then, your memory stopped. Your brain shut down.

It came back up again slowly, like the lights after a movie. You had fallen down, and you were covered in mud—the rain had turned the field muddy.

And then—"Why am I in a field?" And then—"How did I get here?" And then—"I was in the car with Michelle." And then—"Oh yeah, I'm dying." And then—"But still, how did I get here?" And then—"I was drinking." And then—"I don't think I'm drunk, though." And then—"Dear God, how did I get here?"

You could hear the sounds of highway traffic, and way off in the distance, you could see the lights of a Shell station. There was nothing else to be seen or heard. It took... who knows how long it took? Maybe hours. But you eventually walked through the convenience store's automatic doors, heard the mechanical "ping" announcing your arrival. And the few people in the store this late at night (one of whom was a highway patrol officer) all stared at you—wet, muddy, trailing muck in your wake—as you entered the store.

What happened to you, the doctor says after you finish your story, is called dissociative occurrence. It's similar to post-traumatic stress disorder. When you were misdiagnosed and told that your cancer had come back and that you were probably going to die soon, your consciousness just switched off. Your body was still alert and active, but your mind and memory just disappeared. You lost your identity—your entire life—and became an empty vessel controlled by primitive instincts and, perhaps, subconscious desires. You wound up getting out of the car and just running away, until, finally, enough time had passed that you were ready to think about what you had learned. Of course, now that you know you are not actually sick, that the doctor just made a horrible, horrible mistake, it probably won't ever happen again. But there are ways to guard yourself, to make sure it doesn't.

Never drink when you're depressed. Alcohol attacks the frontal lobe first. This is significant.

Don't repress your feelings. Be more expressive. Quit trying to be cool all the damn time, and talk to people when you're upset. "You are entitled to own your feelings," the doctor tells you. Blue Cross/ Blue Shield pays for these profundities.

"We also find that people who have some type of religious faith can usually find strength through that," he adds.

He shrugs. "I'm not really trying to tell you what to do," the shrug seems to say. It's just some friendly advice. You're not crazy. You never were crazy. Perhaps, indeed, the Lord provides.

At the hospital, a week before the appointment with the shrink and two hours from the news that will set off the chain reaction that causes you to seek an appointment with a shrink, you watch as a nurse attaches a needle to the chest catheter of a completely hairless two-year-old girl. The only reason you know she's a girl is because of the earrings in both of her ears. Another nurse is searching your arm for a vein that hasn't been totally demolished by chemotherapy.

"What a good girl," the nurse tells the baby. "And so pretty, too." As you watch the blood getting sucked out of her tube, you flashback to a time when you had a chest catheter. You can remember the fluttering in your chest as they withdrew blood, and, more than that, you can remember the strange taste that came into your mouth when they applied the solution that kept the tube unblocked and clean. What was that taste? Something medicinal, unpleasant. They don't write about that in any of the "Cancer and You" booklets. Maybe the doctors and researchers don't even know about it. It's such a slight thing, after all. Who complains of a funny taste, when there are so many more dramatic things to complain about? Maybe this is a secret that only you know. You and those like you. You and the pretty girl.

It's sad to say, but she's not pretty. She's bald and suffering and, quite likely, dying. This is a Bone Marrow Transplant center, after all. This place treats advanced cancers. She would not be here if the outlook was good. She needs a miracle, but the fact that she is here seems testimony against the very idea of a loving God who might provide such a miracle. Seeing this, seeing her, indicates to you that God's just not home.

Flashing back another year, then two, it seems like you must have been praying quite a bit while you were sick. But maybe not. Is there a difference between praying and just hoping for the best? It's not like you're going into any churches. You don't accept Communion. You don't confess your sins. If you have a relationship with God, it is a casual one. Just a nod and a, "Hey, how's it going? Cure me, please."

No. That's not entirely accurate. There are nights when you stay awake until the early morning, praying for survival, and for the strength to handle it all. Who could forget that? True, in the daylight, it's easy enough to be brave. But at night, alone, in the dark? It's like being in a coffin, isn't it? Was there ever a lonelier feeling? If you couldn't talk to God, you'd have to admit that you were totally by yourself. And that is unacceptable.

You weren't one for prayers before the cancer, though. You'd totally gotten over the lapsed Catholic guilt thing. Remember December of 1997? Shortly before you had to leave school? What was the deal with those two dance students who came to the party after the evening of readings? The evening where you— dressed in black, of course— read your uninspired prose, then retired back to the house to drink Molson Red Jack (do they even make that anymore?) and Cuervo tequila.

Those dancer girls follow you out onto the porch when you go to smoke your cigarette, just to tell you what a great writer you are. And actor, too, for that matter. They'd seen you onstage less than a month before.

"How do you do so much?" the younger girl, the freshman, wants to know. And you answer her, quoting Elvis Costello without any real sarcasm or irony, simply confidence: "Superbly."

Fifteen years ago, you go to Confession for the last time. This is at the West Virginia State Catholic Youth Retreat, the weekend that you begin to decide that you do not really want to be Catholic anymore. You'd heard enough of the nasty rhetoric—abortion was murder and those killers needed to be stopped, rock music was all about worshipping the devil, homosexuals like your Uncle Mike go to hell. The feelings of love and community that had permeated the church when you were younger are dissipating, as you realize that, for those in charge, it is Catholics versus heathens, saved versus hell-bound, us versus them.

You choose Father Dean to hear your confession, because he is young and seems hip. You confess your usual transgression—failure to honor your parents. You even mention the occasional (ha!) impure thought. The priest prays with you, instructs you to keep in mind your parents' wisdom and good intentions at all times, and leaves you with some parting advice:

"It's not hard to do the right thing."

A year before, one day of Catechism class is given over to a young nun who is visiting your parish, The Holy Rosary Catholic Church of Buckhannon, West Virginia. She has come to talk to your class about receiving Holy Orders, about the call to become a priest or a nun. She talks about how she came to know that God had a special plan for her.

And afterward, your Catechism teacher, Dr. Oriyamah, stops you on your way out and tells you that he wants you to seriously consider what the woman has said. "These other guys aren't really into it," he confides. "But I can tell you take this seriously. I can imagine you as a good priest someday." This is a moment of great pride for you. Someone else has confirmed what you have always suspected: Your faith in God is strong, and it shows. You have a seriousness and a devotion that your peers do not. This is, as far as you can see, a very good thing. You are in the eighth grade.

Five years before and three time zones away from that conversation, you're standing in the reception area at St. Monica's Catholic Church in Willows, California. You're wearing the server's uniform of a red cassock and white surplice. It is your first time serving as an altar boy.

You're holding the large metal Crucifix that you will carry down the center aisle, in front of the priests and the other server. You will lead the way. In all of your nine years, you have never been so proud. You have the vague notion that you are now a part of something. Something important, mysterious, and historical—something much larger than yourself. As the people come in, they smile at you, particularly the old ladies who attend every mass and realize that you are new. Their smiles tell you that you are doing a very good thing, but you already know as much.

The processional hymn begins, and you take the first step, knowing that the others will be walking behind you. You hold the Cross high, arms in front of you. Your pace is solemn, but quick. From somewhere off to the left, a flash goes off, and you know your father has just taken your picture. Eventually, this photo will appear in a family photo album. "Billy's First Mass as an Altar Boy." You are nervous, but you know that this is a momentous day.

When you are five years old, Richard, the neighborhood bully, kicks your soccer ball out of the backyard, over the fence, into the parking lot of the church, which is located next door. Richard leaves soon after. You're not allowed to leave the yard, so you go inside.

"Why aren't you out playing soccer?" your dad asks you.

"Richard kicked the ball over the fence," your brother tattles.

Your father looks at you, angry that you didn't come to tell him as soon as it happened. "Go get it."

So you go, but the ball is gone. You look all over, but it's nowhere to be found. Someone must have taken it.

You go over to the house next to the church, where Father McGoldrick lives. He tells you that he hasn't seen the ball, so you start to walk home. As you look at the large white church with the colorful stained glass windows, a thought enters your childish mind, and you walk over to the main steps of the church. The large wooden doors are locked, so you knock. You wait. Knock again.

Defeated, you realize that nobody's home at God's house, and you resign yourself to facing your father empty-handed.

So now you sit, mining the past and struggling to dredge up enough conflict to make yourself into an interesting narrator. You recognize the fact that, when you talk about your own experiences with religion, you sound like you're complaining. In reality, though, you realize that you are in an awfully privileged position. You make enough money to keep food on the table and clothes on your back. Most people seem to like you well enough. You're a moderately successful writer. Your cancer has been gone for years. You're in love with your wife. Aside from the occasional essay written in the second person, you no longer dissociate from yourself.

No doubt, there has been some suffering. But the truth is, you know that the suffering was necessary. It has shaped who you are, caused you to redefine your locus, reprioritize your life. You realize that you have learned a lot from everything that has happened to you, good and bad, and that this awareness has motivated you to try, in some small way, to become a better person. What's more, you know you still love your life. And that's something.

You come to understand that the difficulty does not come from remembering. The memories come easily enough. No, the difficulty is in the longing. Your problem is that you remember a time when you were one hundred percent certain of your convictions. You were unwavering. When you were an atheist, you felt like you understood the world, and your place in it. And when you were a Catholic, everything made sense because everything could be explained as "mysterious ways" on the part of the Lord. Things seemed better, then. What you couldn't understand could at least be accepted. But these days, you can't be sure of anything at all, except that your own uncertainty seems to isolate you.

A wistful Leonard Cohen lyric occurs to you: "I remember when I moved in you / And the Holy Dove was moving too / And every breath we drew was Hallelujah." And you appreciate the sentiment, because you have a similar recollection. And you too feel a similar sense of loss.

This weekend, weather permitting, you'll be sitting on the roof of your favorite bar. Sipping the Corona draft beer you hold in one hand, with the other you will lightly trace the back of your wife's neck while you talk to your friends about the books you're reading and ideas you're having, and you will know that your life is pretty damned good; you have survived a disease many people do not, and the life you held onto is one of remarkable good fortune. And you're going to think something like, "It just doesn't get any better than this." In reality, though, you will know the truth. For all of your blessings—and they are many— you realize that your uncertainty clouds everything for you, and that life could indeed be better, if you were only able to get back to that place when you were confident and filled with a faith you could depend on.

Life on Mars

10.

July, 2012. If we look to the west shortly after sundown, we can see Mars from our front porch, a faint red glow in the twilight. The astronomy website earthsky.org tells us that "Because Earth in its orbit is traveling away from slower-moving Mars and Saturn, these planets will fade in brightness and will sink lower in the evening sky. Even so, these planets will still shine as brightly as first-magnitude stars..." Mars will disappear from view in about a month—right about the time that I have to leave you.

9.

Barsoom— Abbot and Costello went there; Ice Cube fought ghosts there; It's where Dr. Manhattan exiled himself; Yvonne Craig was one of its needed women; its natives grafted Sarah Jessica Parker's head onto her Chihuahua's body; Santa Claus conquered its inhabitants.

8.

I wasn't much of a David Bowie fan, before I met you. Like everyone else, I knew he was a rock and roll legend, and I appreciated the fact that he produced Lou Reed's best albums. But I didn't really appreciate him until that first time we danced together, at that club's "Retro 80's Night." The song was "Modern Love." We were only friends at the time, just getting to know each other, but you said, "It's Bowie—I have to dance." So we put our drinks down and went to the dance floor. That was when things began for us, a decade ago.

7.

In October of 2010, *The Chronicle of Higher Education* ran a story about two researchers—Dirk Schulze-Makuch of Arizona State University and Paul Davies of Washington State University—who proposed sending two humans to Mars on a one-way trip. These hypothetical explorers would go to the red planet and begin construction of a habitat that would, one day, house 150 people, decades after the explorers' own deaths. At the time, we were frustrated at our jobs and with small-minded, small-town living. "So let's go to Mars," I suggested, joking, but also secretly longing to get away from work, away from people, away from the stress of writing and teaching and worrying about tenure and the mortgage and student loans and getting old and realizing I hadn't done anything significant. "They probably wouldn't let us take the cats," you replied, knowing that would cause me to lose interest. You're sensible like that.

6.

Bowie was *The Man Who Fell to Earth*.

5.

You will be living in Murfreesboro, North Carolina next year. I'll be living in Canton, New York. The distance between these places is roughly 700 miles.

4.

We were married on Bowie's 58th birthday. We didn't know it was his birthday when we sent out the "Save the Date" cards, but once we found out, it seemed appropriate, and suggested some type of order or plan to the universe, a glam rock god's Divine Providence.

3.

Depending on where each planet is in its orbit, the distance from the earth to Mars can be anywhere from 34.6 million miles to 249.4 miles.

2.

The physical distance between us for the coming academic year seems overwhelming, but it's really a matter of perspective.

1.

We had not planned on a long-distance relationship at this point in our careers or marriage, but come August, this is where we will be. We both decided, months ago, that this was the right thing to do, but it's getting harder to fathom this time we will spend apart, as my departure date nears. It's not that I'm concerned about our marriage—I know we'll be fine. But I also know that these next few months will be lonely without you. Like sitting in a tin can, far above the moon.

Blastoff.

"Tell my wife I love her very much"—a love that's deeper than the trenches at Noctis Labyrintus, more vast than Olympus Mons.

Harbor Lights Coming Into View

I didn't actually know the old guy, George, very well. Emily and I would see him at our friend Jen's wine bistro, drinking a glass of Merlot while eating his shrimp cocktail. He was a physics professor, and we were both English professors. He liked to talk about John D. MacDonald mysteries and Jimmy Buffett songs, and sometimes he'd tell me things he had already told me multiple times before. I thought it was old age, but his department chair was pretty sure it was his constant drinking. "He's a drunk. He's incompetent. He's gotta go." His department chair was my best friend on campus at that point, so I figured he knew what he was doing when he pushed George into retirement. Shortly thereafter, we heard that his wife had left him and that his kids weren't speaking to him. It seemed the only real friend he had left was Jen. I guess we were his friends too, though as I said, we didn't know him well.

Jen would cook his dinner most nights and try to keep him from drinking too much—although we found out later that he usually drank by himself before he left his house. They would watch *Jeopardy* together, or perhaps an old black and white movie on one of the classic film channels. When we had dinner there, Emily would make a point of talking to him, asking about *A Tan and Sandy Silence* or "A Pirate Looks at Forty."

When he fell down the steps of the bistro that winter night after having just one drink in Jen's presence, he bashed his bald head on the concrete at the bottom. I imagine he must have bled for hours before Russ, Jen's son and my former student, found him. And when I heard a few weeks later that he had finally died, I held it together until we got home, then burst into tears on our front porch. I didn't know the guy, but I had recently lost my job at the same university that he had been pushed out of, and I guess I felt a connection to George. And I worried that I would share his lonely fate somehow.

Emily put her arm around my waist and guided me inside. "Let's just go to bed," she whispered. I apologized to her, told her I didn't understand my own response to the death of someone I didn't really know—just a smiling old guy sitting at a bistro table, really. "It's okay," she said as we got into bed. I told her I thought he was the saddest man I'd ever met. "I know," she said. In the darkness of our bedroom, she put her hand on my cheek and kissed my forehead. George had lost everything, and—I realize now, years after that night—I was afraid that I was in the process of losing everything too. Job, home, wife, purpose. All taken away by people who couldn't imagine the pain such theft causes.

Jen told me she was not welcome at the funeral. We went, saw the administrators who had despised and belittled him wear masks of grief. And then we went to the wine bistro. We had dinner and drank wine with Jen, assured her that she hadn't missed much. And we listened to a CD I had burned for the occasion. UB40's "Red, Red Wine." Crooked Fingers' "New Drink for the Old Drunk." Lou Reed's "My Friend George." George had frequently told us that he wanted Jimmy Buffett's song "Lovely Cruise" played at his funeral. It wasn't played, of course. Those stoical Baptists couldn't indulge a Parrothead's last request. So I put that song last on the CD, and we listened to it more than once—Jen, Emily, and me— as the hours went by and darkness settled in and we drank our wine.

The Essayist's Creed

I.

In some ways, I feel like I have been friends with the essayist Dave Griffith since before we met. If that doesn't make sense to you, then I propose you need to read more personal essays. Granted, as scholars of the form sometimes point out, the essayist's persona on the page is never an exact replica of his mind or personality, but it has been my experience that the essayists I find myself "liking" as personas in a piece of writing generally turn out to be people I like in the "real world," if and when I meet them. This has happened several times, with writers such as Steven Church, Maureen Stanton, Kristen Iversen, and Dinty W. Moore. I guess if you can craft yourself into a personable, amiable "character" in an essay, it stands to reason that you realize what qualities also make for an enjoyable personality when you're actually interacting with other people.

I enjoyed Dave's first collection of essays—*A Good War is Hard to Find: The Art of Violence in America*—a great deal. Of course, there's something to be said for someone who can somehow find thematic links among David Lynch films, Flannery O'Connor short stories, *Star Trek*, Andy Warhol, and the photos of detainee abuse at the Abu Ghraib prison in Iraq. That's just a sharp, creative mind. But there was more to it than that. I appreciated the fact that Dave—and I've met him and he has spent the night in my house, so he's Dave to me, not the less personal "Griffith"—dealt with the pressing political, social, and moral issues of the first decade of the 21st century without resorting to simple-minded, partisan rhetoric. Sure, he was horrified by the detainee abuse, but—unlike a lot of people I knew in 2006, when the book was published—he wasn't satisfied to say that it was just a Lynndie England problem or just a military problem or just a George W. Bush is a bloodthirsty warmonger problem. He was after a deeper truth, something about the culture that could allow such atrocity to happen and then completely disavow it, pretending that what happened half a world away had nothing to do with any of us back at home.

The thing I admired most about Dave's book is that he calls us to look at ourselves even as he peers within himself. He's not content to say that injustice or brutality are the result of "evil people" in opposition to his own innate goodness. He doesn't trust the false dichotomy of "us vs. them" the way so many of us so frequently do. He makes a compelling argument that our important conversations have been corrupted by a reductive Manichaeism, and he urges us to resist such manufactured divisions, as comforting as they may be sometimes. A belief in our own moral superiority is a sin of pride—perhaps the deadliest of the seven deadlies—and, Dave writes, "sets us against each other," causing us to "forever see ourselves as innocent and exceptional—a chosen people ordained by God to rid the earth of evil in a War on Terror."

As the title of the book suggests, he uses Flannery O'Connor's fiction to help illustrate his point. There's no "good and evil" in "Good Country People" or "A Good Man is Hard to Find." There are just flawed people whose encounters with the grotesque help them to eventually discover Grace—the Grace promised by the God O'Connor (a devout Catholic) believed in.

A lesser writer might have left it at that, but Dave goes deeper, exploring his own religious faith without embarrassment, apology, or a cocoon of irony. When he speaks of his own Catholicism and the way his faith influences how he perceives the world, his sincerity jumps off the page. Not in a proselytizing way, but just in an attempt to explore and explain his own thoughts, how his mind wrestles with these ideas. He's not writing a polemic—although his opinions are in there, sure—but he is interested in moving beyond an overly-simplified dialectic where two sides, convinced of their own virtue, simply shout at each other.

As a lapsed Catholic who married into Lutheranism with some ambivalence, I admired such a firm statement of his own conviction. I only knew two churchgoers when I was in graduate school and Dave's book was released. One of them was my wife, and even she felt uncomfortable talking about religious doctrines, instead focusing on religion's influence on the culture she lived in and the literature she studied as well as the sense of community she experienced when she went to church.

Me? Oh, I hid behind that familiar line, "I like to think I'm spiritual, but organized religion is corrupt and isn't for me." I avoided talking about the issue, which was relatively easy. Even my most thoughtful, philosophical friends tended to avoid talking about their personal belief systems, preferring abstractions and theories about faith to actual discussions about what they believed. The truth was, I did believe in something larger than the individual, the community, the world that we live in. I did believe in God.

But I couldn't express such belief. Not the way Dave could. Not then.

II.

Recent polls suggest that nine out of ten Americans believe in God. Most—but by no means all—of these believers identify themselves as Christians. However, according to the Barna Research Group—an Evangelical Christian polling firm—only 9% identify faith as the most important thing in their lives. An Associated Press/ GFK poll indicates that nearly eight out of ten Americans believe in Angels. A National Geographic poll conducted in 2012 found that 77 percent of Americans believe that there is evidence to suggest that aliens have visited earth (only one in twenty said that, in the event of coming into contact with an alien, they would "try to inflict bodily harm"; I guess that's a pretty good statistic). About a third of Americans believe that the destruction of the World Trade Center was "an inside job." Three out of ten Americans believe Bigfoot is real.

I guess you have to believe in something. Maybe most of us need to believe in something bigger than ourselves that can affect or even control our fate. As Bob Dylan sang during his Evangelical Christian phase, "Well, it may be the devil, or it may be the Lord/ But you're gonna have to serve somebody."

III.

I served as an altar boy when I was a kid, in two churches—St. Monica's in Willows, California and Holy Rosary in Buckhannon, West Virginia. My sixth grade CCD teacher served the Lord by telling us that children in Africa were starving because children in America weren't Praying the Rosary. My eight grade CCD teacher served the Lord by telling us that Martin Luther protested Vatican opulence and split off from the Catholic Church because "he wanted to be a big shot." He also suggested that I might serve the Lord by becoming a priest someday—a suggestion I took quite seriously. If you believe in Catholic doctrine—and I did, deeply—what's a few decades of celibacy and poverty compared to the eternal rewards that await you? If I hadn't developed this nagging agnosticism in high school, I might be a priest today.

My seventh grade CCD teacher—my neighbor, an obstetrics nurse who was then ten years younger than I am now—served the Lord by telling me once that I should abstain from sex until marriage, but that if I did have sex, I should make sure to use a condom, regardless of what the Vatican says. And though the Pope and the American Conference of Catholic Bishops and William Donahue would say she was completely wrong to say such a thing to a 12-year-old, my own moral compass tells me that she was the one spiritual authority during my middle school years who told me something that was right and true.

IV.

My wife thinks that, at some point, I must have said or done something that the campus minister found insulting, that led her to try to sabotage my career. Indeed, according to the provost and president, the minister claimed that I had complained to her that there was "too much prayer and such" at certain campus events. That I had never said such a thing—*would* never say such a thing—was beside the point. She said I said it. And she had God on her side. So.

Aside from accusations of Godlessness, the campus minister felt that the creative nonfiction essays I wrote illustrated my depravity—specifically, an essay I had written years before I'd even heard of the school (and that I had discussed with university officials when I interviewed for the job) demonstrated my lack of moral fiber, according to her. The essay recounts a Key West vacation where my wife and I found ourselves the only monogamous couple staying in a bed and breakfast that was otherwise rented out entirely by swingers—most if not all of whom were older than our parents. It employs profanity as it describes our shock as an elderly couple began to have sex in the clothing-optional pool right in front of us. It uses humor to explore our discomfort, but it concludes on, I think, a humane note. Though my own sex life is quite conventional—twelve years of heterosexual monogamy with the woman I'm married to—it seems to me that those whose sex lives may seem "bizarre" to those outside their relationship deserve to have love and happiness too, if they can find it.

In short, an essay about love cost me my job at a Christian university. And though it may seem obvious to you that one's job at a Christian university might be jeopardized by writing frankly about unconventional sexualities, I can only say that I took people at their word when they told me that I was free to live my life as I saw fit—I was not required to sign any statements about my own faith or attend a church—and to write and publish my work. I had faith, you can say, that the people who hired me would treat me with honesty and respect.

But that's not what happened. I had to leave my home to take a job fourteen hours away, while my wife stayed behind for the year and continued to work with the people who had, effectively, driven me into exile for my heresy.

I am convinced that the campus minister didn't really understand the essay's central point about love and tolerance— she encountered language and descriptions that she found objectionable and couldn't get past them to see the larger context. I can't really be angry about that—it's not her fault if she didn't "get it"; in fact, it could be that the writing wasn't clear enough for the larger context to be comprehended. I can acknowledge that; her misreading of the essay might be the result of my flaws as an essayist. But here's what I am angry about: the woman has never said a word to me about her objections to the essay. She has never expressed concern for the state of my soul. She never indicated that she would pray that I would see the error of my ways. Instead, she decided that, to serve the Lord, she would campaign to have a popular teacher (I had been nominated for the school's awards for both teaching and scholarly productivity) fired. That losing my job might mean losing my house, losing my dignity, and perhaps even losing my marriage—the most important thing in my life—did not give her pause.

This may be bitterness talking, but I cannot for the life of me see a person who could cause such pain as an agent of a loving God. And the administrators who sacrificed academic freedom on their campus because they feared that a controversial faculty member might have a negative impact on fundraising strike me more as agents of Mammon.

V.

I have friends who are atheists, but I am not an atheist myself. I get down on organized religion—the Catholics who want to restrict access to birth control, the Evangelicals who think some types of love need to be "fixed" through debunked and unscientific "therapies," the Baptists who caused my wife to cry at least once a day for an entire month as they were trying to hurt us. But the fact that human beings are stupid, prideful creatures prone to sin is no reason to abandon God. In fact, Dave Griffith writes, "For O'Connor, God's providence was realized not despite our sins, but through them. Removing sin from life—or fiction—meant essentially cutting yourself off from the possibility of grace."

I want grace very, very badly. I want to be cleansed of my iniquities and purged of the hatred I have in my heart. I want to be forgiven—not for writing a "dirty essay," but for the rage that fills me when I hear the essay described in such terms. And I want to have the capacity for forgiveness as well.

So to find grace, it seems to me that I have to believe in it. More than that, though, I see evidence of the divine every day. In the small kindnesses that people afford each other. In my friendships. In music and art. And, most frequently, in literature.

If you're looking for the sublime, read Andre Dubus's "A Father's Story," which ends with its narrator, horse breeder Luke Ripley, talking to the God he has worshipped his entire life, explaining why he has allowed his unconditional love for his daughter to lead him into sin by covering up a fatal crime that she has accidentally committed:

So, He says, you love her more than you love Me.

I love her more than I love truth.

Then you love in weakness, He says.

As You love me, I say, and I go with an apple or carrot out to the barn.

Or consider Tolstoy's Ivan Ilych, who learns at the end of his life that superficial pursuits have kept him from truly living his life and whose self-centeredness has tormented his family. On his deathbed, he has "revealed to him that though his life had not been what it should have been, this could still be rectified." He apologizes to his family, and tries to ask for absolution: "He tried to add 'forgive me,' but said 'forgo' and waved his hand, knowing that He whose understanding mattered would understand."

And of course, there's the grandmother in O'Connor's "A Good Man is Hard to Find." A woman who, face-to-face with the man who intends to murder her, suddenly realizes how connected we all are to each other: "Why you're one of my babies," she tells the Misfit as she faces her own death. "You're one of my own children!"

These stories, I am convinced, reveal truth, just as I tried to reveal truth in my essay about love and sex. I have faith—not in a vengeful God who sends hurricanes to punish gay people, but in a God of mercy and beauty. The God revealed in the works of Dubus, Tolstoy, O'Connor, and others. These are works that convince me that there is a certain divinity to be found in all who live, placed there by a loving creator who wants us to understand that we deserve to love and be loved.

VI.

I don't pray in public for the same reason I don't write in public, the way you sometimes see young poets scribbling in their moleskins in a Starbucks or writing professors pecking away at laptops in the hotel lobby at the annual conference of the Association of Writers and Writing Programs. These activities are sacred, and are not merely performance. Something about the guy who prays over his Sbarro pizza at the mall food court or the woman who works on her chapbook while sipping her soy latte suggests to me that being seen demonstrating this commitment is more important than the commitment itself. I could be way off-base on this. I probably am. Nevertheless, that's always my kneejerk reaction to seeing such a public display of something that I only do in private.

VII.

But when I pray, I pray with fervor and sincerity. I clarify my thoughts, focus on this communication between myself and my audience—as I do when I write, although in this case, the audience is a force that I can't quite understand, and won't understand in this lifetime. A force misunderstood by most who claim to know It—particularly by those who claim that their personal relationship with this force makes their judgment in all matters practically infallible. I don't want to sound like one of those people who say "I'm spiritual, but not very religious." Not anymore. I am religious, but I'm comfortable with ambivalence. I can't claim to know much more than the fact that O'Connor is right—Manichean dualism is nonsense, and any belief system that turns us prideful and compels us to look down on another person is a false belief system. But that is something I know for certain.

So here's my prayer. My Essayist's Creed, if you will.

Dear God, cure me of this arrogance. Allow me to resist being judgmental without sacrificing my own moral code. Permit me a greater understanding of the world You created and the people who inhabit it—especially those whom I am most inclined to judge, in my weaker moments. Lead me not towards prejudice or bigotry, and if I must hate—as, occasionally, I have to admit that I do—do not allow that hate to overwhelm me, do not let its fires consume me, and give me the strength to resist the urge to act on such hate. Above all, remind me each day that every human life has a spark of Divinity, placed in it by You, and that all people are worthy of attention and love. For these things I pray to you, O Lord, forever and ever, Amen.

Dream Child: A Reverie

After Elia

C hildren love to listen to stories about their elders when they were children; they find it fascinating to know that their parents, grandparents, aunts, uncles, and other older relatives once had lives like theirs, spent their summers riding bicycles and playing "Marco Polo" at the public pool, whiled away rainy afternoons watching movies and playing videogames, spent holidays and vacations with the extended family. It was in this spirit that my daughter crept between my wife and me as we sat together on the couch to hear about her great-grandparents— Oscar and Ruth Isaacson and Kenneth and Ruth Cooper on her mother's side, Billy and Marguerite Garrett and William and Eleanor Cook on mine—and other members of the family who are no longer with us, for one reason or another. Of my wife's paternal grandparents, there is nothing terribly entertaining to say. They were already quite old by the time Emily knew them, and the stories she tells of the overheated Chicago apartment they lived in, or the boiled chicken they always seemed to eat, are unpleasant without being grotesque or scandalous, which make them uninteresting to our Josephine, who enjoys picking up spiders and would like for us to allow her to get a pet boa constrictor. Kenneth and Ruth are more interesting to her, I think because Emily has more stories to tell about them—tales of learning to bake with Ruth, or learning to respect intellectual achievement from Kenneth, the history professor and textbook author. Kenneth's study was a massive library, with some books well over a hundred years old even when Emily was a girl. It was a reliquary for knowledge, a place where all of the secrets of the world could be discovered. In hindsight, it was probably the place where Emily decided that she too would devote her life to scholarship and books. And though Josephine enjoys hearing these tales of her mother's girlhood, I think she prefers hearing about my experiences in my extended family. This might be because we don't have as many pictures of my relatives in the house or in the photo albums. It might also be that she—young as she is—has already intuited that I do not have the same fondness for my extended family that my wife has for hers. I neither dislike nor like these people all that well—some of them are nice enough, others are not, but none of them are people I tend to interact with very much beyond a Christmas card exchange and Emily's annual letter updating the family on Josephine's progress in school and any developments happening in our careers. But this was not always the case. I used to spend my summers in New Mexico, staying with my father's mother and step-father (Joseph Bradley, my dad's dad, had been dead several years by the time I was born). The Garretts—particularly Nana—were quite kind, but the smoke from their constantly-burning cigarettes would get into my eyes and throat. The combination of smoke with dry desert air would lead to massive nosebleeds for me, the kind that would go on for 30 or sometimes 45 minutes and would sometimes leave me exhausted afterwards. So I would try to spend as much time outside of the house as possible, taking golf lessons with my cousins—Katie, Joey, and Chip—and my siblings, Steve and Molly. After the morning golf lesson, we would go back to my cousins' house for a quick lunch before deciding how to spend the afternoon. We might go back to the Country Club to spend the rest of the day in the pool, or we might get on bicycles to ride to the convenience store several miles away to buy Cokes and Charleston Chews and *Garbage Pail Kids* ("What are *Garbage Pail Kids*?" Josephine asked. Before I could think of how to explain, Emily said, "They were these silly cards that dorky kids used to waste money on." To correct her and say, "Actually, they were stickers," would only confirm my nerdiness to both my wife and daughter, so I don't). This was how we spent every summer, from June until the end of July. Then, we would return to our home in West Virginia in time for my mom to load us into her van and drive us to New Hampshire to see her mother, Nana Cook, as well as my Uncles Brad and Michael, Brad's wife Fran, and my cousins Sue and Kate whose father, my mom's brother Billy, drowned while saving his daughters from an undertow when we were kids. Nana Cook had had a history of psychological problems even before the loss of her eldest son, but she became particularly vicious after he died, telling anyone who would listen—children and adults alike— that my cousins were responsible for their father's death. Stories about Nana Cook fascinate Josephine, and I have to be careful not to make my grandmother sound like some type of witch or other agent of supernatural evil—Josephine has already inherited her father's obsession with horror movies, and I don't want to give the girl nightmares. More importantly, I don't want her to fear the mentally ill or have a two-dimensional understanding of this woman in our family who caused and experienced great pain. Also, I don't want her to think that I disliked these trips to Nana Cook's; it was quite the opposite. We would go fishing on Brad's boat, go to the movies while Nana took my mom shopping, go to the beach with Fran. But most of all, I liked Nana Cook's house for the basement. Nana Cook and her husband, Papa, had moved into the house when I was little, and I imagine Papa might have had some ambitions for the finished basement that went unrealized after his health started to decline. He managed to put a pool table down there, but the ornate wet bar went unstocked, and the area—stretching the entire length of the house—was unfurnished save for a desk and an office chair in a room off to the side, as well as the washer and dryer installed behind folding closet doors. Nana got rid of the pool table after

Papa died, but I still loved to play down there, in my own private Batcave ("Because your father was a nerd," Emily pointed out, an observation to which Josephine giggled her ascent). I conspired to stay on Nana's good side, so she would leave the house to me in her will. I would install the largest, most state-of-the-art computers in this basement, to assist me in my war against crime as surely as Batman's computers helped him. I would even wall off the doorway that led down to the basement and install a fireman's poll in the bathroom that contained the trap door that we tossed our laundry down. At this idea, Josephine loudly reiterated her mother's accusation, "Dad, you're such a nerd," and something about this accusation made me think of the Superman comic books I loved as a kid, and love to this day. Specifically, it called to mind the Alan Moore-written story "For the Man Who Has Everything," in which the villainous Mongul uses mind control to fool Superman into thinking that he still lives on Krypton, and is married and raising a son, Van-El. It's a trick, designed to put the Man of Steel in a catatonic state and trap him in his most cherished fantasy. Of course, Superman eventually realizes he has been tricked (with a little help from Batman, Robin, and Wonder Woman), and he lets go of the illusion, difficult as it is, telling his beloved Van, "You're my son. I was there at your birth and I'll always love you, always, but… but Van, I… I don't think you're real." Why did this come back to me at my daughter's accusation of nerdiness? And why did I look at this child, who looked at once like my wife and like someone I'd never met before, someone whose features grew faint the more I tried to focus on them, as she said, "I am not of Emily, nor of thee, nor am I a child at all." And then, I remembered the phone call from the fertility clinic 15 years before, the voice on the other end of the line telling me I didn't need to bother providing a third sample—the chemotherapy treatment had made it so that there was no way I would ever father a child. And

I remembered going to take a shower so that no one in the house would hear me crying over the water. And I remembered how Emily and I decided we would adopt a baby when I was 36 and she was 34, once we were settled in our careers and were certain we could afford the expense. But then I lost my job, and we had to live several states apart—sleeping in the same bed during summers and on holidays and some weekends—in order to continue to pursue our career goals as English professors. And I realized I was not sitting on a couch at all, that I didn't even own a couch anymore, and that neither Josephine nor Emily was beside me. I was alone in this dark apartment. My daughter, my Little Lamb, is nothing; less than nothing, and dreams. She is what might have been, but maybe, maybe, she is also what still might be. I'm older than 36 now, but there might still be time. So she waits upon the tedious shores of Lethe, until the time she can join us and be called Josephine.

You're a Wonder

Hippolyta created Wonder Woman out of clay, though I'm not sure why. Artistic expression? Boredom? Did she often sculpt babies? Were there earlier, imperfect sculptures, made as Hippolyta learned her craft, not granted life by the goddess Aphrodite? I imagine there were. This woman, this queen, beloved by her sister-subjects on Paradise Island, but so painfully alone. So she sculpted a little clay brood to delight her in a utopia where life could be enjoyed but never created.

I'm lonely myself. If we can't live in the same place, my dear—and at the moment, we can't full-time—I think I'd like to sculpt you, then ask Aphrodite to do me a solid, allow me to create you and breathe life into you, perhaps with a kiss. Although that sounds more fairy tale than comic book. But she's the goddess of love—maybe she'd go for that.

I'd bring you to life, then regard you with a smile and a, "Hey." And you'd reply, "I've missed you," and you'd put your arms around me.

But what would you say next? You have the wisdom of Athena, so I imagine it might be something like, "Shakespearean scholars think about Shakespeare as but one of a cluster of playwrights in the period. Knowing this — and thinking about the broader question of 'Who were all of these men who wrote the plays?' — means that Shakespearean scholars are looking for a different set of information and operating with different assumptions about the fundamental concepts in the issue."

But then again, maybe not. You're an intellectual, true, but you're also a woman of passion. It's unlikely that you'd mark our reunion with scholarly discourse. You'd be more excited to see me, I think.

"Fuck me with your huge cock."

Tempting, but no. In the 12 years we've been together, you've never issued such a greeting. I'm confusing you with pornography.

"Shall we open a bottle of wine?"

That suggestion raises some problems too. You are, after all, made of clay, and clay dries out quickly even without the dehydrating effect of alcohol. Hippolyta and her daughter never had this problem, but as we drink I notice you begin to look a bit ashen. I spray you with one of the water bottles we use on the cats when they fight; this helps for a little while, but the reality that we do not have much time begins to sink in. You are turning white and beginning to crumble; so, for that matter, am I. It's unavoidable—the reality that underlies this ridiculous fantasy. We're human, and crusty, dry decay is what awaits us. You are not the only one here who came from—and will return to— dust.

In reality, neither of us can sculpt, let alone create life from clay. All we can do, I guess, is write. We can at least hope that my essays and your scholarship will give us some form of immortality. But on days when we're too hungover or uninspired to get any writing done, let's resist the temptation to sit in front of the TV or spend the day focused on chores or stressing about all the money we don't have. Let's enjoy this time we have together. Let's get out of here, away from wasteful, banal distractions, and have some adventures together. If we can't procure an invisible jet, we can take the Corolla, which just got an oil change and has new windshield wiper blades.

Self-Similar

"In our own splintered and less credulous age, the belief that
literature can communicate a sense of universality beyond
singularity or authorial presence has lost much of its strength.
But the power of literature, it seems to me, still lies in its
imaginative ability to imply a realm beyond our grasp; by
transcending the limitations of reader, character, and society,
it can give us an awareness of our human mutuality." (James
McConkey)

It's dangerous to make sweeping statements about universal
truths. Anyone who has studied human history knows that
"universal truth" has often been used to justify oppression and
even genocide. Claims about what "everybody knows" or an
intuitive sense of "absolute justice" should be taken with a grain
of salt—and the people who make arguments based on their
perceptions of what is universally true should be immediately
distrusted and resisted at all costs. It's especially dangerous
when you convince yourself that you or the politician you favor
genuinely knows what is best for everyone.

But if I argue against essentialism and policy that comes
from intuition rather than reasoned debate, don't presume that
this means that I feel like we're hopelessly separated from one
another, unknown by and unknowing of others. Don't imagine I
think that we're all isolated beings, alone in the universe except
for the subjective truths and moralities that our cultures impose
upon us. While I think it's important that we question ourselves,
our beliefs, and our society, I think—in fact, I think I *know*—
that there are some things that we have in common, regardless
of where in the world we've come from. I believe the words of
the world's first essayist, Michele de Montaigne, who wrote

that "Every man has within himself the entirety of the human condition."

Our understandings of religion, justice, and morality might depend entirely upon where and when we live, but I think most human beings experience joy. They experience anger. They experience sorrow. And I suspect human beings everywhere give expression to those feelings. We are able to learn. We have epiphanies. We experience catharsis.

We are made of cells—the buildings blocks of life. These tiny fractals contain the information that makes us *us*. On a microscopic level, we're all quite similar to each other indeed.

As someone who failed and had to retake almost every math class from eighth grade Algebra on, I'm probably the least qualified person in the world to talk about Benoit Mandlebrot and his ideas about *The Fractal Geometry of Nature*. I hated math as a kid, and—until very recently—found that I had very little use for it as an adult. But Mandlebrot and his ideas about fractals fascinate me. A fractal, Mandlebrot tells us, is "a rough or fragmented geometric shape that can be split into parts, each of which is (at least approximately) a reduced-size copy of the whole." That is to say, Mandlebrot tells us that in nature as well as in theoretical mathematics, the small part of the larger thing—the fragment of the geometric shape, the particle, the cell, the grain of sand, the speck of dirt—resembles and represents the larger whole.

The lapsed Catholic in me imagines God creating the first fractal in man and declaring, "Let us make man in our image, after our likeness." But if you and I don't share religious beliefs, I hope we can at least come together on the mathematics. I can't help but feel like we'd be better as a species if we tried to imagine each individual as a self-similar component of the larger human race. I know I feel like I'd be a much better person if I endeavored to always think of you, me, and even the Osama bin Ladens and John Wayne Gacys of the world as fractals, fundamentally identical parts which represent a similarly identical whole. The knowledge that we are, for all practical purposes, the same should be enough to keep us from hating each other despite the differences we think we perceive in each other. Or at least it seems that way to me.

Traditional Thanksgiving Recipe

1 lb. ground turkey
¼ cup shredded parmesan cheese
¼ cup Cabot's Habañero Cheddar
1 tsp of chili powder
1-2 minced garlic cloves
dash of salt and ground pepper
1 bag of frozen tater tots
1 bottle of barbecue sauce
3-4 horror movies—the cheesier, the better

Begin by trying to be traditional. Invite friends from your graduate program in English over for a big Thanksgiving meal. Your fiancée will make a turkey, you can make the stuffing and mashed potatoes. Serve some green beans, too. Buy a pumpkin pie. This is, after all, your first Thanksgiving since you moved in together, just a month and a half before your wedding. You are Very Serious Grown Up People now, people who can be trusted to pay their bills on time and maybe even raise a kid. And this meal, you think, will somehow prove it.

Of course, neither of you really likes turkey—oh, sliced thin for a sandwich it can be fine, but huge chunks of dry meat? Even smothered in gravy, about the best you can say is that the gravy makes the meat less bland. You know there are people who claim that their own turkeys are succulent and flavorful, but you suspect that they are fucking liars and that there is no way to turn turkey into an enjoyable meal. You can try to move stuff around on your plate so the turkey gets mixed up with the stuffing and the potatoes and the green beans, but doesn't that just seem wasteful and silly? There's always that flavorless chunk of bird flesh ruining every mouthful of delicious carbohydrates.

Your friends eat enough to be polite, but are really more interested in drinking the wine and beer you bought for the occasion while they talk about Marcel Proust or Emily Dickinson or Jorge Luis Borges or Ron Jeremy. Drink your own Pinot Noir slowly as you try to clean up the kitchen—you don't want to be the drunkest person at your own party. Not this early in the evening, anyway. But you despair, and think about drinking even more, as you realize you'll be eating leftovers for the next several days.

In the ensuing years, try to find new ways to do Thanksgiving as you move across the country multiple times. Go out one year. Order a pizza another. When you're both vegetarians, do up a vegetable stir fry, or just eat sides at someone else's house. All are better than the usual Thanksgiving dinner, but it doesn't quite feel *special*. Well, except for the part where you drink beer in the afternoon while watching football. And then, when you both agree you're not really into football, drink beer in the afternoon while watching movies.

And though beer in the afternoon is always enjoyable, something seems off. Thanksgiving should be more notable than your typical day on vacation. You long for the pleasures that tradition provides. Without some way to mark the day as unique, an annual holiday to be celebrated as opposed to just a day off from work, it feels like you and your wife are missing out on something.

Develop your own Thanksgiving tradition accidentally, after you both go back to eating fish and fowl when you learn that soy products have a negative interaction with a prescription drug you have to take every day. Agree that neither of you wants to cook and eat a whole turkey, but that turkey burgers might be tasty. Acknowledge that stuffing and green beans, while good enough at a typical Thanksgiving dinner, don't really appeal to either of you, and that while potatoes are delicious, they're much better in "tot" form than mashed. Decide that you're not really interested in being around other people—that you'd prefer to spend this day together alone. Also, conclude that the day's movies will all be horror films, beginning with *Friday the 13th, Part 3*—the DVD of which actually came with 3D glasses that will allow you to enjoy the original theatrical 3D effects from the comfort of your own couch.

You or your wife should divide the ground turkey in half. Mix half the turkey with the Parmesan cheese, and half with the habañero cheddar—your wife is not as into spicy food as you are. Divide the chili powder, garlic, and salt and pepper between the two turkey and cheese mixtures. Form each mixture into two patties. Grill on a grill pan, turning frequently, until cooked through. This will take about 15-20 minutes.

In the meantime, make the tater tots. Directions are on the bag.

Realize as you take your first bite that this is the best burger—turkey or otherwise—that you have ever eaten. It's juicy and spicy and more flavorful than you ever imagined turkey could be. Dip your tater tots in the barbecue sauce—dip the entire burger in the sauce too, for that matter. Wipe your hands on a napkin before putting on your 3D glasses and pressing "Play" on the remote control.

Compliment your wife on this amazing recipe that is, mostly, her creation. Smile when she replies, "Thank you, baby." Watch the film's opening sequence, as Jason stalks and kills Harold and Edna. Watch your wife's face as the teenagers load themselves into the van and the hippie guy—who looks like Tommy Chong and is clearly too old to be hanging out with these kids—hands them a joint that seems to leap from the screen into your living room. Laugh, both with and at her hysterical response.

As you finish your meal, lean back on the couch and put your arm around your wife. Let her snuggle into your chest, but be careful not to crush the arms of her 3D glasses.

"We're so fucking cool," she'll sigh.

"We should have a kid," you'll say in agreement.

Repeat this process, once a year, every year—alternating movie choices and maybe someday no longer talking hypothetically about a kid—for the rest of your life.

Ham's Lesson

To avoid an argument, we headed east, my wife and I, on Highway 68. We drove away from Canton and towards Sevey's Corners in order to find some evidence of a life that had ended 20 years before, hoping that the experience might result in something to write about.

Ham Ferry had been something of a legendary figure in this area of the Adirondacks, holding court in the small hamlet's only bar—the bar that they named after him, I'm pretty sure—Ham's Inn. This place, according to the website of the organization Traditional Arts of Upstate New York, was "[Ham's] natural setting and the spot where he held listeners rapt for hours on end." He was a raconteur, telling stories and tall tales involving naturally-gifted hunting dogs, North Country wild life, and teasing the game warden who was a bit too excited to exercise his authority over the plain-spoken rural hunters in his bailiwick.

I first became aware of Ham Ferry when Emily and I purchased a CD titled *Funny Men of the Adirondacks*, which collected recordings of these old men of rural upstate New York telling their stories. While all of them had some charm, I found myself most drawn to Ferry's. Perhaps because he had died much earlier than most of the other men—in 1994, the same year that I moved to the North Country for the first time—he seemed even more anachronistic. He sounded like someone who lived in and described a world that ceased to exist shortly before I was born.

Upstate New York is still pretty wild in many respects; the state has done a good job protecting the natural, untouched beauty of the Adirondack State Park. You don't have to travel too far on any given hiking trail to get the feeling that you've left humanity behind. You can still find the old fire towers, where watchers would stand and enjoy the broad, expansive views of valleys filled with spruce, pine, and fir trees, and you can enjoy the same view yourself and marvel at the natural beauty and sense of history these towers provide. But similarly, you don't have to walk back for very long to return to a world of Wal-Marts and McDonalds and IMAX movie theaters.

Ham Ferry lived in a North Country of scattered general stores, locally-owned taverns, and old men sitting on barstools telling stories to an amused and grateful crowd of beer drinkers. I can picture these people—hunters and their wives, maybe— sitting in Ham's Inn, glasses in hand. A cloud of smoke hangs in the air. Outside, the wind is whipping and the snow is accumulating on the ground, but the people inside are warm from the wood stove and the alcohol they have consumed. All but one are silent, their eyes on skinny, bald Ham Ferry as he concludes the story about the old-timer who ran out of shot and wound up loading his muzzleloader with cherry pits, and the deer he shot who nonetheless got away. How the old hunter, in the same woods a year later, came across a most amazing sight. "It was that buck he shot at before, the fall before," he says in his quiet, raspy voice, "and the cherries were growin' out on both sides of it." The sound of laughter fills the bar, and Ham smiles as he lifts his own glass to his lips.

It's not that I want to live in Ham Ferry's world, mind you. I love those IMAX movie theaters. But it's a nice place to visit, in old photographs and audio recordings. And though some efforts have been made to preserve what we have left of it, I fear that that world is in danger of being lost forever.

I don't know quite what my wife and I were hoping to find when we made our pilgrimage to Sevey's Corners. I was pretty sure Ham's Inn had been closed for years, and I doubted we'd find anybody who had known the man. I guess, maybe, we might have hoped to find a bar like the one Ham frequented. Maybe find an old man sitting at the bar, bullshitting about his own glorious and hilarious past. The one thing I did know is that we had been in the process of moving from one apartment to another, and that this was the first move we'd ever made where we didn't get into a fight about something. We've moved together six times in our twelve year relationship, and I've found that whether it's frustration over getting the cable guy to hook up our Internet or stress about the money spent on U-Hauls and security deposits, we usually find something to snap at each other over at some point during the process. That we hadn't so far this time was cause for some celebration, but there was also the nagging fear that the fight was just around the corner. That suddenly one of us would find a water-damaged box of books or a broken heirloom, shout "Goddamn it!" in response, jangling the nerves of the other to the point that we'd both stop putting in the effort to be pleasant while dealing with the stresses of the move.

So, when she realized she had not hooked the washing machine up properly—she emerged from the basement soaked from head to toe, face red, clearly on the verge of crying—I very gently suggested, "You know, we've been working really hard. Why don't we go out to lunch and then drive around for a while?"

This is what Emily and I tend to do in moments of stress or fatigue. Get in the car with a map and a sense of an eventual destination, always on the lookout for the strange and photograph-worthy. With the likes of David Bowie, Kanye West, and Sleater-Kinney providing the soundtrack on various mix CDs we burn for each other, we have travelled all over the Midwest, rural South, and Northeast. I have a photo of Emily in front of Sumner, Missouri's giant concrete goose, Maxie. Emily has a picture of me standing beside what some say is the world's largest pecan (although the residents of Seguin, Texas dispute this claim, insisting that their pecan is larger). We have visited a museum dedicated to presenting the "evidence" for Creationism, where we both struggled to be polite to the nice but dangerously wrongheaded people working there.

We drank beer in a bar called The Drunken Monkey with a man who introduced himself to us by declaring, "I played 36 holes of golf today. On meth." We have found ourselves in a tavern watching *Wheel of Fortune* and eating chicken gizzards while the woman who worked behind the bar patiently explained to us—the strangers who had just wandered into her bar— just what a chicken gizzard is. We once met a guy with a face spiderwebbed by broken blood vessels who kept coughing into his handkerchief as he told us about working construction when Disney built Epcot Center.

In Hemingway's "Hills Like White Elephants," the girl asks her lover, "That's all we do, isn't it—look at things and try new drinks?" But when Emily talks about that story, she always adds, "But she says that like it's a *bad* thing." Emily and I have driven all over this country, stopping in various small town bars, and we inevitably wind up talking to strangers with stories to tell. As one guy talks about hunting rabbits or another woman tells us about how her girlfriend has turned into a jealous psycho, as Johnny Cash plays on the jukebox or a baseball game plays on the TV mounted behind the bar, our fingers inevitably find each other under the table. We squeeze each other's hand, and that squeeze seems to say, "I'm having an awesome day. And I love you."

In fact, when we renewed our wedding vows a couple of years ago, each of us promised the other that we would never grow tired of looking at things and trying new drinks.

It turns out there wasn't much to look at in Sevey's Corners, and there wasn't a place to try any type of drink, old or new. Of course, I knew we weren't going to find Ham himself—he was long dead. But I guess maybe, now that I think about it, I was hoping to find Ham's doppelganger—another old man with interesting stories who could hold court while Emily and I listened. I'm not a gregarious guy myself, and though I write essays, I'm not always comfortable talking about myself. But I'm always curious to hear what other people have to say—especially when they've had experiences and lived lives that aren't anything like my own. The stories they tell might be true, but then again, maybe not. But I always find such conversations instructive. They remind me that the world is bigger than I sometimes think it is, and that other people—strangers I'll never see or hear from again—are living their remarkable lives as I go on with mine.

I have ambivalent feelings about the inevitable forward march of time. Without progression, we can't have progress, and we'd be stuck cooking all of our food over open flames and voting for men like George Wallace and Jesse Helms. I don't want that. But I also don't want to grow old and die. And I don't want my wife to grow old and die. I want to freeze us in a perpetual present, where we are both happy and energetic. I don't need for us to be teenagers or twentysomethings or in the best shape of our lives—it's not vanity, you see. But I don't want one of us to become immobile or comatose or dead. I don't want us to break each other's hearts like that.

But if time insists on moving forward, and the universe insists on denying us a fountain of youth, we'll do just that. So I'd like to make sure I don't squander the time allotted to us by fighting or forgetting to be grateful for what we have in each other. We have been together for twelve years and married for almost ten, and she's still my favorite person to be around. It's easy to be married to her—she's supportive and agreeable and has an excellent sense of humor. I think she would probably say that she finds me supportive and agreeable and that my sense of humor isn't too absurd or annoying. We have a satisfying sex life—I've never felt particularly attracted to another woman, and if she has been overwhelmed with lust for another man she has had the good sense to refrain from telling me about it.

It's a powerful and incredible thing, this love. But it will end eventually, as everything does. And people likely won't be sitting in a bar in some small town telling the story of the Adirondack Boy who brought his Chicago Girl back to the North Country. And even if there was some Ham Ferry to tell the tale, he would die eventually too.

We'll continue to have arguments. We'll take each other for granted sometimes, and we'll continue to let life's frustrations distract us from that which actually matters. I don't think that can be avoided. But what we can do—all we really can do, it seems to me— is remember that we periodically need to get in the car together with music we can agree on and a couple of sodas or bottled waters. Gas up the car, pick a direction. Look at things, try new drinks, and do our best to find something to write about the experience.

We did find Ham Ferry's grave in a tiny cemetery in the nearby town of Gale, but it wasn't anything terribly impressive— just a grave, next to the grave of his wife. No pithy quote on the tombstone. No impressive statuary. Not even any flowers. It was just a site that marked that someone had lived, but does not live anymore. We got out to take pictures, but the gnats and blackflies were swarming all around our faces, so we got back in the car pretty quickly and slapped at the bugs that had managed to get in while the doors were open.

"So what now?" I asked as Emily backed the car up.

Braking to shift into drive, Emily turned to me and said, "That bar in South Colton had Molson Canadian on tap."

"Works for me," I replied as I put my hand on her knee. We drove north on Highway 56, anxious to see what and who we'd find when we got to our destination.

What the Wedding Photos Don't Show

We spent hundreds of dollars to hire Nola to take hundreds of pictures at our wedding, but we never look at them. Which is kind of a shame—she was an excellent photographer, Nola. But images—like language—are insufficient when it comes to telling the truth about things.

Our wedding photos don't show the way you smiled at me when we met at a party in 2002. They don't show us surrounded by candles in my old apartment on our first Valentine's Day as a couple, or your naked back as you sat up in my bed the next morning, glancing over your shoulder at me. They don't show how I thought "I love her" for the first time when you gave me that look.

They don't show us setting up the bookshelves in our first house on Sunrise Drive. They don't show us drunk in the living room, dancing while my Reel Big Fish concert DVD played. They don't show the way you laugh when I exclaim "Motherfucker!" as you place the tiles on the Scrabble board in the exact place I need you to *not* place them.

They don't show us in the hot tub in our honeymoon suite, but that may be for the best.

They don't show me taking your hand in the car while you cried when we pulled away from our house in Missouri for the last time, on our way to Florida. They don't show the way you talk about sex to distract me when I'm close to having a panic attack on an airplane. They don't show the unspeakable dread I felt when that jackass in the pick-up truck rear-ended us, totaling our car and leaving you—only momentarily, but it felt like forever— unable to answer me when I asked "Are you okay?" They don't show the way you put your arm around my waist to help me up to our second floor apartment after the surgeon took a chunk out of my thigh.

They don't show the times I stormed out of the house after a terrible argument, leaving you to cry alone. They don't show the time you told me that I'd made you so angry earlier that day that you'd thrown up. They don't show us on the side of the highway—out of gas, each of us feeling it was the other's fault—and how we both silently concluded under the July Florida sun that this was the fight that would finally lead to our divorce.

They certainly don't show how we forgive each other everyday. Or how we make each other laugh when you call me "Scumbag" and I call you "Needledick." They don't show that I'm the only person in the world who knew to buy you the Collected Works of Thomas Middleton for Christmas, or that you're the only one in the world who knew to buy me the *All-Star Family Feud* DVD for my birthday.

Scrunching up our faces and saying "Grrr" to each other when we pass in the halls at work. My head in your lap while we watch TV. Holding hands in the mall even though we're old. You touching my leg while I'm driving. The way you turn on your side while still asleep and put your arm across my chest in the morning.

The photos show our wedding and reception, and I guess in a sense they show how much I love you, since they capture me committing my life to you. But they don't show how deeply and profoundly I *like* you; they don't show our marriage. It's too weird and wonderful for a mere photograph—or, for that matter, an essay— to express.

Epilogue: On Soap Operas
or
We Read and Watch Our Stories In Order to Live

(Canton, NY, 2013)

After a lengthy absence from the show due to his declining health, John Ingle's last appearance as *General Hospital* patriarch Edward Quartermaine was broadcast on September 11, 2012. Ingle had been something of an institution on *General Hospital*, having played the role of the scheming, cantankerous businessman since 1993 (with the exception of a couple of years when the role was recast with another actor). A retired high school teacher whose drama students included Richard Dreyfuss, Barbara Hershey, and Albert Brooks, Ingle was reportedly an avuncular presence on the set, willing to help younger actors learn their craft and older actors hone their skills. When he died five days after the broadcast, on September 16th, his former co-stars sang his praises on social media. Steve Burton, who played his grandson Jason Morgan, tweeted, "A great husband. A great father. A great friend. A great actor. A great man. We love you John." Billy Warlock, who played his other grandson A.J. Quartermaine, tweeted "Today is the saddest day of my life. My friend and mentor John Ingle passed away last night. I'll miss him more than words can say." In the obituary released by ABC, Leslie Charleson, who played his daughter-in-law Monica Quartermaine and may have shared more screen time with him than just about anyone else still on the show, said, "He was genuinely interested in people and everything that was going on... his dressing room door was always open, and many of us would find our way there to pick his brain and, in turn, he would lend an ear and offer his wisdom." The show's executive producer Frank Valentini noted, "In our brief time working together, I have enjoyed getting to know a great man who embraced life, cherished what he did and, most of all, loved his family. He is already truly missed by the *General Hospital* family."

Of course, these are things people say when someone dies. And when the deceased is a celebrity with even a minimal amount of fame, the cynical among us sometimes imagine that the condolences and expressions of grief from other celebrities might be, shall we say, less than sincere. These people pretend to experience emotions for a living, and much of their appeal comes from audiences identifying with them. Public mourning— especially in a venue like Twitter—can seem self-serving.

I think, though, that these comments are heartfelt, that the loss expressed by these people was genuine. Or maybe I just like to think it, because I like the story of the retired teacher who found success as a full-time actor and who never lost his gift for instruction, and whose insights and advice were appreciated by his co-stars and unofficial students. You can call me sentimental if you wish, but I want to believe that these TV stars appreciated their fallen friend, and recognized—as I did when I read the news of his death—that this death mattered, that this life mattered, and that this loss was significant. "We tell ourselves stories in order to live," Joan Didion wrote in "The White Album," and this story of the soap star teacher and his appreciative and adoring students was one that I found myself desperate to believe in.

Having cancer was a terrible experience, but I find myself grateful for the life I've lived since my final radiation treatments in 2000. My cancer had been especially pernicious, recurring twice—once in 1998 after initial chemotherapy treatments, and then again in 2000 after aggressive chemotherapy and an autologous bone marrow transplant. I hated the chemo, of course, but radiation was far worse for me. It left me nauseous and fatigued to the point that I couldn't work, but not so exhausted that I slept peacefully. More than that, it left me depressed and lethargic. I could have gone out, but didn't. I might have interacted with friends, but I usually chose solitude. Most of the time, I sat on the couch, playing *Tomb Raider II* on a borrowed Playstation until I felt like I couldn't see straight. Or listening to Warren Zevon's *Life'll Kill Ya* album—Zevon's stripped-down, slowed-down cover of Steve Winwood's "Back in the High Life Again" suggested a sense of melancholic delusion in the song's speaker that is absent from Winwood's original, and the song became my theme song for a while there, as I sadly promised myself that I too would soon "Drink and dance with one hand free" and "Have the world so easily" once I was back in the high life I belonged in. Or, occasionally, watching *General Hospital*. But not often. I didn't have cable in my apartment at that point, and this was before the days of a high-speed Internet that allowed us to watch our stories on our computers.

I do know that at this point Edward Quartermaine was frequently something of a villainous figure, and that in 2000, he was working hard to keep young Emily Quartermaine from the boy she loved, Zander Smith. The understanding was that Edward was too old to understand the pure love the two shared, and too much of a blueblood to allow his granddaughter to associate with someone as common as the street-smart Zander—a "hooligan," Edward frequently, cantankerously charged. Even Edward's wife, the saintly Lila Quartermaine, thought Edward heartless for trying to stand in the young lovers' way. Seldom brought up was the fact that Zander and Emily met because he was her drug dealer, and he took her hostage and kidnapped her in order to escape from the police when he was suspected of murder.

People who do bad things are often forgiven on soap operas, if they repent their evil ways and test well with audiences (this is why there are so many rapists-turned-romantic-leads on daytime dramas). The actor who played Zander, Chad Brannon, was good looking and had chemistry with Amber Tamlyn, the actress who played Emily. So they became a young supercouple, and Edward—the only character to voice the completely sensible objection that this young woman was clearly suffering from Stockholm syndrome and needed to be protected from her captor-cum-boyfriend—wound up looking like a bitter old fuddy-duddy.

Several characters on General Hospital have had cancer. Monica Quartermaine developed breast cancer in the 90s. Her adopted daughter Emily developed breast cancer as well about a decade later. Super-spy Robert Scorpio survived colon cancer. Josslyn Jacks had cancer in both of her kidneys. At different times, things looked dire for these characters, but they all lived to love another day.

Angelina Jolie—the actress who played Lara Croft in the movies based on the *Tomb Raider* videogames—had both of her breasts removed after learning that a defective gene left her with an 87% chance of developing breast cancer. She will, presumably, live to see her children grow up.

On September 7, 2003 Warren Zevon died of mesothelioma nearly ten months after his final live performance on *The Late Show with David Letterman*, where he ended his set not with his famous crowd-pleaser "Werewolves of London" but with the less-famous, but better, "Roland the Headless Thompson Gunner." After his diagnosis, Zevon lived to see the births of his grandchildren and the release of his final album, *The Wind*.

Nine years and four days after Zevon's Letterman appearance, Edward Quartermaine appeared on General Hospital for the last time, speechless save for four words uttered to his daughter Tracy; five days after that, the cancer he had been fighting for all of 2012 finally killed John Ingle.

When I'm teaching literature, I always make a point of re-reading the stories, poems, and essays I assign my students, even when I have read them dozens of times in the past. I always discover something important that I had forgotten. Sometimes, my wife has to correct me when I say something like "I've never seen a Georgia O'Keefe painting in person before" by saying, "Yes you have—you couldn't stop talking about O'Keefe after our visit to the Chicago Art Institute." Stanley Kubrick is my favorite filmmaker, but I still haven't seen *Barry Lyndon*. I keep meaning to read more James Joyce—I know I ought to be familiar with more than just *Ulysses* and "Araby," but I never seem to find the time.

I've seen *Sorority Babes in the Slimeball Bowl-a-Rama* more than once, though.

"As a writing man, or secretary," E.B. White wrote in "The Ring of Time," "I have always felt charged with the safekeeping of all unexpected items of worldly and unworldly enchantment, as though I might be held personally responsible if even a small one were to be lost." And I guess that's part of what motivates me too. To write, and to write about stuff that mattered to me, even if it strikes some as silly or lowbrow. The world changes fast, and life as we know it changes before we have time to register. Just think of the changes John Ingle—born in 1928—saw in his lifetime. The development of the Interstate Highway System. Televisions in every home. The rise of the Internet. The world that he died in was not the same world he was born in.

So it will be for me. So it is for all of us.

While it's dangerous to live in the past, to give in to nostalgia's deceptive pull, I think we're well-served by making an effort to remember the world as it existed, as we perceived it at the time. Holding onto what was real keeps us rooted to who we have been, and reminds us of the world—or, perhaps more accurately, worlds—we have lived in. The history books will remember the presidents and the captains of industry. Neither Nabokov nor Twain will ever go out of print. Scholars and culture critics will make sure we remember the *Citizen Kanes* and *The Wires*.

But who is going to remember the *One Life to Lives*? Or the *Howard the Ducks*? Or the *Tic Tac Doughs*? These things were part of our cultural landscape for a time. People worked hard on them, and surely their efforts and the work that resulted ought to be remembered in some way. They might not have had the lasting impact the works of high art are supposed to have, but they mattered to a lot of people, who labored on them or experienced them as an audience that cried, laughed, or played along at home.

And who, for that matter, will remember me?

The hospital was overrun with dying patients—the villainous Jerry Jacks and his accomplices, Dr. Ewen Keenan and Joe Scully Jr, had poisoned Port Charles's water supply. Many, including the Quatermaines' beloved cook, Cook, had already died.

For some reason a few residents seemed unaffected by the toxin—Alexis Davis, Josslyn Jacks, and Tracy Quartermaine were all inexplicably healthy. An examination of Tracy's blood showed that, somehow, she had antibodies that counteracted the venom. In fact, a smitten Joe Jr. had given Tracy the antidote that Jerry had given him to guard against the toxin's effects, but nobody knew this at the time. All they knew was that the doctors at General Hospital had been able to synthesize a single dose of the cure, and would not have time to develop more before the citizens of Port Charles began to die from Jacks's treachery.

While the heroic doctors—Monica Quartermaine, Steven Webber, Patrick Drake—debated what to do with the single vial of the antidote, Tracy broke into her sister-in-law, Monica's, office to steal it. The cure came from her blood, she reasoned, thus she would be the one to decide who among the thousands of sick citizens would get it.

She had her father, Edward, brought to the hospital. He didn't say a word as orderlies pushed his wheelchair into the crowded emergency room, and he was silent as Tracy spoke to him in his private room, where she produced the purloined vial and said, "I want you to drink this."

The conversation that immediately followed Tracy's instruction can only exist our imaginations, but when we next saw Tracy and Edward, they were holding hands, "I love you, Daddy," she said.

Slowly, with apparent difficulty, he replied, "I love you too," then left his mouth open in a slight gasp, as if he might be overcome with emotion, as she leaned forward and kissed his cheek.

And then, Tracy left the room to find Patrick Drake, to tell him that Edward had insisted that the antidote be given to the good doctor's sick daughter.

"No one has ever watched a soap opera and said, 'My God! I can't believe that happened!' I doubt anyone's life has ever been changed by something he or she saw on a daytime drama."

I wrote those words at some point in 2003 or 2004, as I was composing the very first essay that I would later publish. That essay got me some positive attention—publication, as I said, and a "Special Mention" in that year's Pushcart Prize anthology of small press publications and "Notable Essay of 2005" in *The Best American Essays* collection. Its success likely resulted in my first academic job, too, after I finished my Ph.D. work. I've taken a lot of pride in that essay over the years, but now I wonder if I might have gotten a few things wrong.

I didn't say out loud, "My God! I can't believe that happened" when John Ingle was wheeled onto the set of *General Hospital*. In fact, I had read beforehand that he would be appearing after a months-long absence—perhaps for the final time, his family had said in interviews. I knew he had been sick, even suspected—though I didn't know for sure—that he might have had cancer (he'd been treated for a melanoma on the top of his head a few months before, which meant that he was always conspicuously wearing a hat during his subsequent appearances on the show). But I was still surprised to see just how much he seemed to have aged. The last time he had been on, he was able to portray the same opinionated, belligerent, yet ultimately family-oriented character he had been playing for decades. Now, he was in a wheelchair, thin and gaunt, and apparently unable to speak.

Of course, he did speak. He said, "I love you too." Not merely "I love you," which would have spared him the effort of uttering an additional syllable and been quite moving on its own. But "I love you too." In character, as Edward, this line was directed towards his daughter, Tracy. But I think—or I choose to believe—that this was also the actor himself, addressing his fans, those people who had watched him play a schemer, a curmudgeon, a husband and a father for years. "I love you too," he told them, anticipating how they would respond once his cancer had finally claimed him, as he must have known it soon would.

Did watching John Ingle's final scene as Edward Quartermaine change my life? Not exactly. But it did remind me how frail and fleeting our lives actually are, and that's a lesson that can't be driven home hard—or frequently—enough, I think.

We go to bed, and my wife falls asleep before me. We're both college English professors, and we both have a habit of reading something not work-related before we go to sleep—nothing we're going to try to teach in the morning. For Emily, that usually means a short story from someone like Andre Dubus or Ann Beattie. It sometimes means that for me too, but it also sometimes means flipping through the latest *New Yorker*. Or humor by the likes of Al Franken or Jack Handey.

But tonight, maybe I go into my office and grab an *Incredible Hulk* out of my collection. Say, issue 376, which came out when I was in the eighth or ninth grade and features the "Gray Hulk" fighting the "Green Hulk" inside a space created by Dr. Bruce Banner's fractured mind. Their goal is to kill each other, but as a reader, I know that none of them—Gray, Green, or Banner himself—will survive unless the three personalities are integrated into a healthy, complete whole. This was one of my early lessons in psychology, although I'd seen a similar process of fragmentation and reintegration on *Another World*, when innocent housewife Sharlene Frame developed the alter ego "Sharly," a prostitute who cavorted with a U.S. congressman.

I could read this and remember what it was like to be a kid excited by the adventure and psychological horror of radiation-spawned monsters fighting for supremacy. Or maybe I'll pick up *The Making of* Star Wars, and remind myself of how thrilling I found these movies, and how inspiring it is to realize that, when he was my age, George Lucas was not yet famously successful—there's hope for me yet. Or maybe I'll crack open my copy of *Worlds Without End: The Art and History of the Soap Opera*.

Whatever I decide, I will fall asleep thinking about these things that I've loved in the past, these things that I love even now, and that I will likely continue to love in the future. Once upon a time—when I was 22 years old—a doctor told me there was only a 40% chance that I would live to see 27. I'm 38 now. I have been very lucky, and I hope I don't sound too selfish when I say that I hope this streak of good luck keeps going for a very long time.

If I'm really lucky, my wife will groggily roll over, put her hand on my chest, say good night and tell me she loves me. I, of course, will tell this woman I have been with for the past twelve years, "I love you too," and I'll fall asleep grateful and content.

Acknowledgements

I'm really grateful to the following magazines and journals for publishing early versions of the essays in this manuscript.

"Prologue, or On Soap Operas: The Bald and the Beautiful" originally appeared in *The Bellevue Literary Review* as "The Bald and the Beautiful."

"And Never Show Thy Head By Day Nor Light" was originally published in *Burleseque Press*.

"How We Got Our Dog" was originally published in *Bluestem*.

"Fear" was originally published in *Full Grown People*.

"Julio at Large" was originally published in *Brevity*.

"Cathode" and "Dream Child: A Reverie" were originally published in *Sweet: A Literary Confection*.

"ABVD PGA Champ" was originally published in *Flashquake*.

"Best Thing" was originally published in *Rawboned*.

"As One Might Expect" was originally published in *Ars Medica*.

"Marked" was originally published in *Cleaver*.

"Chrononaut" was originally published in *The Jabberwock Review*.

"First Thing" was originally published in *Full Grown People*.

"Peace Through More Power Than a Locomotive" and "You're a Wonder" both appeared in the chapbook *Tales of a Multiverse in Peril*, published by Urban Farmhouse Press. "You're a Wonder" was also published at *Bending Genre*.

"What the Survey Doesn't Say" was originally published in *Antique Children*.

"Dislocated" was originally published in *The Normal School*.

"Life on Mars" was originally published in the online version of *The Pacifica Review*.

"The Essayist's Creed" was originally published in *Passages North's* online "Writers on Writing" feature.

"Traditional Thanksgiving Recipe" was originally published in *Full Grown People*.

"Ham's Lesson" was originally published in *Sundog Lit*.

"What the Wedding Photos Don't Show" was originally published in the online version of *Opium*.

And I need to thank a few other people too.

Michael Piafsky has been a great friend and editor for the past twelve years. If this book is any good at all, it's largely because of what I've learned from him.

Jill Talbot's feedback and encouragement on several of these essays was similarly invaluable.

I can't say enough nice things about all of the literature and creative writing professors I've had the good fortune to study with. Sid Sondergard, Thomas Berger, Kerry Grant, Ghislaine McDayter, Paul Lehmberg, John Smolens, Pat Okker, and Maureen Stanton were particularly influential.

Ken Wolfskill is the most loyal friend I've ever had, although Craig Clark and Christian Exoo come pretty close.

Ned Stuckey-French has been a consistent source of wisdom and support.

Christopher Murphy has been my best friend since high school and his wife Noelle Murphy has been my best friend since college. I know that you can't technically have two "bests," but I couldn't choose between them. Their friendship and love meant a lot to me when I was sick, and they continue to mean a lot to me to this day.

My wife Emily Isaacson made me promise shortly after we started dating that I would never write about her. Obviously, I broke that promise, and I keep breaking that promise, but she loves me anyway and has even grown to enjoy being a muse/ character. As David Bowie tells Tilda Swinton in the video for "The Stars Are Out Tonight," "We have a nice life."

Finally, my friend and mentor Natalia Rachel Singer. She was my very first creative writing teacher and my academic advisor. She introduced me to the personal essay in a creative nonfiction workshop back in the fall of 1997, shortly before I got sick, and my life hasn't been the same since. I owe her a debt I can never repay, but I'll dedicate this book to her in an attempt to do so.

About the Author

W illiam Bradley is the author of *Tales of a Multiverse in Peril!*, a chapbook collection of story/essay hybrids published by Urban Farmhouse Press. *Fractals* is his first full-length book.

His work has appeared in a variety of magazines and journals including *The Missouri Review, Brevity, Creative Nonfiction, The Chronicle of Higher Education, Fourth Genre,* and *The Bellevue Literary Review.* He regularly writes about popular culture for *The Normal School* and creative nonfiction for *Utne Reader.*

He lives in Canton, New York, with his wife, the Renaissance scholar and poet Emily Isaacson.

Visit www.williambradleyessayist.com

CPSIA information can be obtained
at www.ICGtesting.com
Printed in the USA
BVHW051714060722
641478BV00014B/165